MathFlare

Name: ______________________

Class: ___________

Teacher: ______________________

Introduction

As parents and educators, we recognize the pivotal role mathematics plays in shaping a child's academic journey and future success. Yet, the path to mathematical proficiency can often seem daunting, fraught with challenges and complexities. That's where the transformative power of MathFlare Workbooks shine through, illuminating the way forward with clarity, precision, and purpose.

Introducing MathFlare Workbooks – a beacon of guidance, a testament to excellence, and a catalyst for achievement. Crafted with meticulous care and expertise, MathFlare Workbooks stand as paragons of educational excellence, designed to nurture young minds, ignite a passion for learning, and develop a deep-rooted understanding of mathematical concepts.

Picture this: your child eagerly delves into the pages of Mathflare Workbook, greeted by a step-by-step guide illuminated with vivid examples that demystify complex mathematical concepts. With each turn of the page, they embark on a journey of discovery, encountering thoughtfully curated practice questions that reinforce learning and hone problem-solving skills. And when they unveil the answers to those very questions, a sense of accomplishment blossoms within them – a tangible reward for their hard work and dedication.

But MathFlare Workbooks are more than just tools for learning; they are pathways to comprehension, fostering a deep-seated understanding of mathematical concepts through a sequential, logical flow. From fundamental principles to advanced problem-solving strategies, every chapter builds upon the last, ensuring a robust foundation upon which future knowledge can be constructed.

As parents, we yearn for nothing more than to see our children thrive, to witness the spark of inspiration ignited within them as they conquer academic challenges with confidence and poise. MathFlare Workbooks serve as partners in this noble endeavor, offering not just practice questions, but the keys to unlocking a world of opportunity.

And for teachers, MathFlare Workbooks stand as invaluable allies in the quest to cultivate mathematical proficiency in the classroom. With answers readily available, instructors can focus on guiding and nurturing their students, confident in the knowledge that MathFlare Workbooks provide a solid framework upon which to build.

In the pages of MathFlare Workbooks, we find not just the promise of academic excellence, but the seeds of a brighter tomorrow. So let us embrace the power of mathematics, let us champion the journey of learning, and let us pave the way for a generation of young minds poised to shape the world. With MathFlare Workbooks as our guide, the possibilities are infinite, and the future, bright.

Table of Contents

MathFlare
MATH WORKBOOK
2
Step by Step Guide and Essential Practice with Answers
Addition Subtraction
Multiplication
Place Value and Expanded Notations
Geometry
MathFlare Publishing

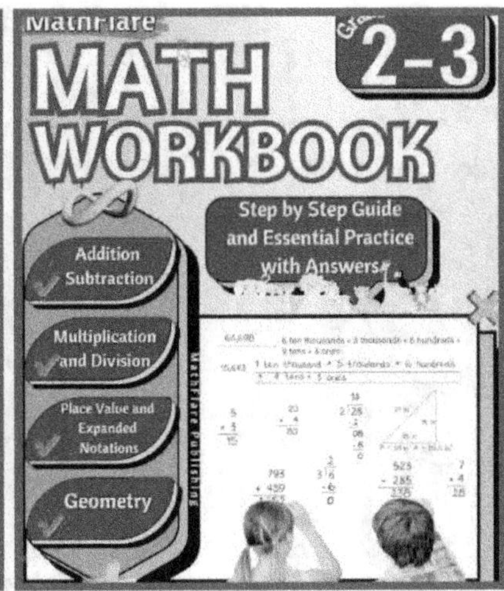
MathFlare
MATH WORKBOOK
2-3
Step by Step Guide and Essential Practice with Answers
Addition Subtraction
Multiplication and Division
Place Value and Expanded Notations
Geometry
MathFlare Publishing

MathFlare
MATH WORKBOOK
3
Step by Step Guide and Essential Practice with Answers
Multiplication and Division
Decimals
Place Value and Expanded Notations
Fractions and Geometry
MathFlare Publishing

MathFlare
MATH WORKBOOK
1
Step by Step Guide and Essential Practice with Answers
Counting and Numbers
Addition and Subtraction
Place Value and Expanded Notations
Understanding Time
MathFlare Publishing

MathFlare
MATH WORKBOOK
1-2
Step by Step Guide and Essential Practice with Answers
Counting and Numbers
Addition and Subtraction
Place Value and Expanded Notations
Understanding Time
MathFlare Publishing

MathFlare
MATH WORKBOOK
3-4
Step by Step Guide and Essential Practice with Answers
Addition Subtraction
Multiplication Division
Place Value and Expanded Notations
Fractions and Geometry
MathFlare Publishing

MathFlare
MATH WORKBOOK
4
Step by Step Guide and Essential Practice with Answers
Addition Subtraction
Multiplication Division
Place Value and Expanded Notations
Fractions and Geometry
MathFlare Publishing

MathFlare
MATH WORKBOOK
4-5
Step by Step Guide and Essential Practice with Answers
Multiplication Division
Place Value and Expanded Notations
Fractions and Geometry
Unit Conversion
MathFlare Publishing

MathFlare
Grade 5
MATH WORKBOOK
Step by Step Guide and Essential Practice with Answers
Multiplication Division
Place Value and Expanded Notations
Fractions and Geometry
Unit Conversion
MathFlare Publishing

MathFlare
Grade 5-6
MATH WORKBOOK
Step by Step Guide and Essential Practice with Answers
Multiplication Division
Place Value and Expanded Notations
Fractions and Geometry
Units and Statistics
MathFlare Publishing

MathFlare
Grade 6
MATH WORKBOOK
Step by Step Guide and Essential Practice with Answers
Integers and Statistics
Arithmetic and Pre-Algebra
Fractions and Geometry
Ratio and Percentage
MathFlare Publishing

MathFlare
Grade 6-7
MATH WORKBOOK
Step by Step Guide and Essential Practice with Answers
Arithmetic and Pre-Algebra
Ratio, Percent Proportion
Geometry
Statistics
MathFlare Publishing

MathFlare
Grade 7
MATH WORKBOOK
Step by Step Guide and Essential Practice with Answers
Pre-Algebra
Ratio, Percent Proportion
Geometry
Statistics
MathFlare Publishing

MathFlare
Grade 7-8
MATH WORKBOOK
Step by Step Guide and Essential Practice with Answers
Pre-Algebra
Ratio, Percent Proportion
Geometry and Cartesian Plane
Statistics
MathFlare Publishing

MathFlare
Grade 8-9
MATH WORKBOOK
Step by Step Guide and Essential Practice with Answers
Pre-Algebra
Ratio, Proportion and Percentage
Linear Equations
Geometry and Cartesian Plane
MathFlare Publishing

MathFlare
Grade 8
MATH WORKBOOK
Step by Step Guide and Essential Practice with Answers
Pre-Algebra
Percentage
Linear Equations
Geometry
MathFlare Publishing

Multiplication and Division

Multiplication

Multiplication is an easy way of adding numbers together quickly. Instead of adding the same number repeatedly, we use multiplication to find the total much faster.

For instance, rather than adding 2 + 2 + 2 + 2 + 2, we can multiply 2 by 5 to get the same result: 2 x 5 = 10.

Here, the first number (2) is called the multiplicand, second number (5) is the multiplier. The answer we get, in this case, 10, is called the product.

Let's think of multiplication as repeated addition.

Take 2 x 5, for example. It means adding 2 together five times, which we can illustrate as: 2 + 2 + 2 + 2 + 2 = 10

Multiplication can also be visualized as groups of objects. Imagine we have 2 groups, each containing 5 oranges.

To find the total number of oranges, we multiply the number of groups (2) by the number of oranges in each group (5):

2 groups of 5 oranges = 10 oranges

Expressed as multiplication: 2 x 5 = 10

In summary, multiplication offers various ways to approach it: through repeated addition or by envisioning groups of objects. It's a powerful tool that makes solving math problems much quicker and more efficient!

We can also use the following table to quickly remember multiplication facts. The intersection of two points shows the product of two numbers.

For instance, the product of 5 x 6 = 30, or 6 x 5 = 30.

	1	2	3	4	5	6	7	8	9	10
1	1	2	3	4	5	6	7	8	9	10
2	2	4	6	8	10	12	14	16	18	20
3	3	6	9	12	15	18	21	24	27	30
4	4	8	12	16	20	24	28	32	36	40
5	5	10	15	20	25	30	35	40	45	50
6	6	12	18	24	30	36	42	48	54	60
7	7	14	21	28	35	42	49	56	63	70
8	8	16	24	32	40	48	56	64	72	80
9	9	18	27	36	45	54	63	72	81	90
10	10	20	30	40	50	60	70	80	90	100

Let's solve problems from exercises:

$$
\begin{array}{r}
20 \\
\times\ \ 4 \\
\hline
80
\end{array}
\qquad
\begin{array}{r}
10 \\
\times\ \ 7 \\
\hline
70
\end{array}
$$

Commutative Property of Multiplication

The commutative property of multiplication is a special rule in math that tells us the order of the numbers being multiplied doesn't affect the result.

For instance, let's take 2 x 5. If we switch the order of the numbers, multiplying 5 by 2 instead, we'll still end up with the same answer: 2 x 5 = 10, or 5 x 2 = 10.

So, whether we multiply 2 by 5 or 5 by 2, we get 10. That's the commutative property of multiplication in action!

Division

Division is like the opposite of multiplication. It's all about sharing or distributing items equally among a certain number of groups or people.

When we divide one number by another, we're essentially splitting a number into equal parts. We're figuring out how many groups of a certain size can be made from that number.

For instance, let's divide 20 by 4.

When we divide 20 by 4, we're essentially asking, "How many groups of size 4 can we make from 20?"

Now, there are several parts or terms involved in the division process:

- Dividend: This is the number being divided, which in this case, is 20.

- Divisor: This is the number we're dividing by, which is 4.

- Quotient: This is the answer we get after dividing. It tells us how many groups of the divisor can be made from the dividend. In this case, the answer is 5.

So, when we divide 20 by 4, we found out that 5 groups of 4 can be made from 20.

Let's solve problems from exercises:

$$
\begin{array}{r}
18 \\
2\overline{)36} \\
-2 \\
\hline
16 \\
-16 \\
\hline
0
\end{array}
\qquad
\begin{array}{r}
5 \\
2\overline{)10} \\
-10 \\
\hline
0
\end{array}
$$

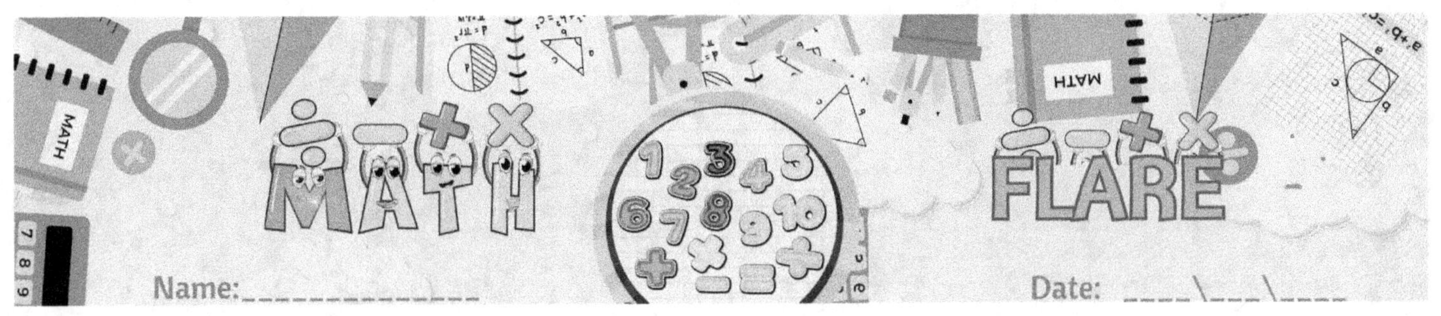

Multiplication by 2

1. 6
   × 2

2. 5
   × 2

3. 2
   × 4

4. 3
   × 2

5. 2
   × 8

6. 2
   × 2

7. 7
   × 2

8. 9
   × 2

9. 1
   × 2

10. 2
    × 7

11. 8
    × 2

12. 2
    × 6

13. 4
    × 2

14. 2
    × 3

15. 2
    × 5

16. 2
    × 1

17. 2
    × 9

18. 5
    × 2

19. 2
    × 2

20. 6
    × 2

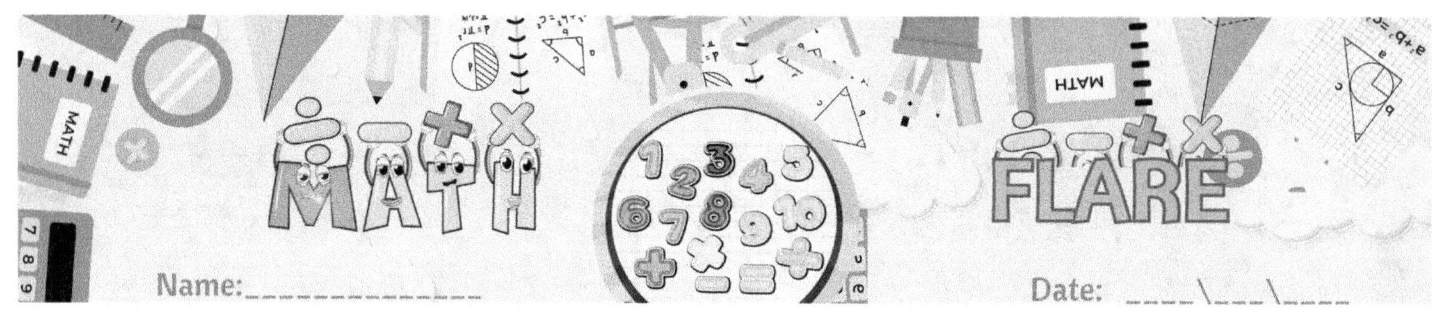

Multiplication by 3

21. $\begin{array}{r}2\\ \times\ 3\\ \hline\end{array}$	22. $\begin{array}{r}4\\ \times\ 3\\ \hline\end{array}$	23. $\begin{array}{r}3\\ \times\ 3\\ \hline\end{array}$	24. $\begin{array}{r}3\\ \times\ 8\\ \hline\end{array}$
25. $\begin{array}{r}3\\ \times\ 5\\ \hline\end{array}$	26. $\begin{array}{r}3\\ \times\ 1\\ \hline\end{array}$	27. $\begin{array}{r}3\\ \times\ 7\\ \hline\end{array}$	28. $\begin{array}{r}9\\ \times\ 3\\ \hline\end{array}$
29. $\begin{array}{r}6\\ \times\ 3\\ \hline\end{array}$	30. $\begin{array}{r}3\\ \times\ 9\\ \hline\end{array}$	31. $\begin{array}{r}7\\ \times\ 3\\ \hline\end{array}$	32. $\begin{array}{r}3\\ \times\ 4\\ \hline\end{array}$
33. $\begin{array}{r}5\\ \times\ 3\\ \hline\end{array}$	34. $\begin{array}{r}3\\ \times\ 2\\ \hline\end{array}$	35. $\begin{array}{r}8\\ \times\ 3\\ \hline\end{array}$	36. $\begin{array}{r}3\\ \times\ 6\\ \hline\end{array}$
37. $\begin{array}{r}1\\ \times\ 3\\ \hline\end{array}$	38. $\begin{array}{r}6\\ \times\ 3\\ \hline\end{array}$	39. $\begin{array}{r}8\\ \times\ 3\\ \hline\end{array}$	40. $\begin{array}{r}3\\ \times\ 4\\ \hline\end{array}$

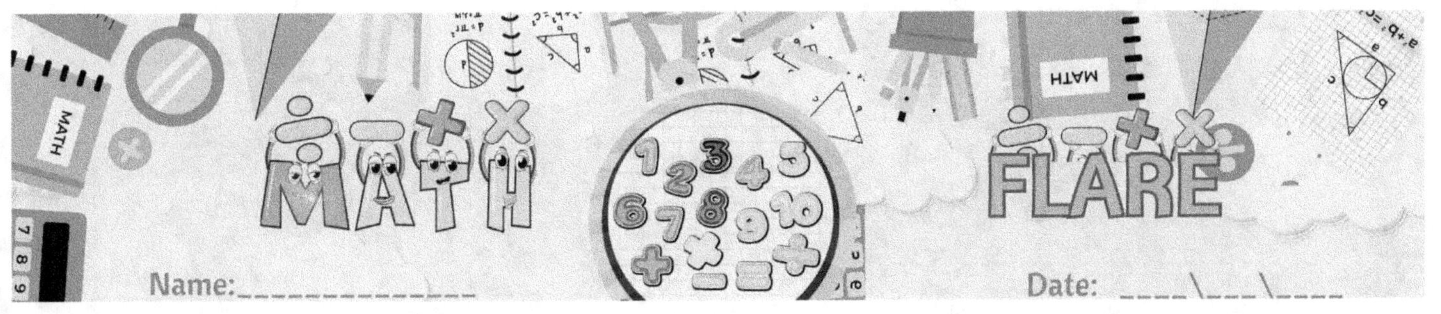

Multiplication by 4

41. 8 × 4	42. 3 × 4	43. 4 × 6	44. 5 × 4
45. 4 × 4	46. 4 × 2	47. 4 × 7	48. 9 × 4
49. 1 × 4	50. 2 × 4	51. 6 × 4	52. 4 × 5
53. 4 × 9	54. 4 × 3	55. 7 × 4	56. 4 × 1
57. 4 × 8	58. 5 × 4	59. 4 × 4	60. 1 × 4

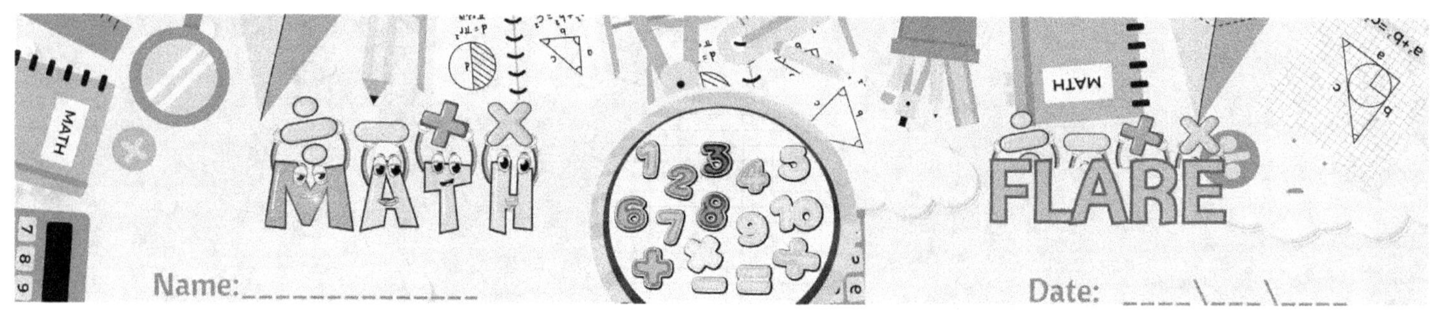

Multiplication by 5

61. 5 × 3

62. 9 × 5

63. 5 × 5

64. 5 × 2

65. 4 × 5

66. 5 × 6

67. 7 × 5

68. 1 × 5

69. 8 × 5

70. 2 × 5

71. 6 × 5

72. 5 × 7

73. 3 × 5

74. 5 × 8

75. 5 × 9

76. 5 × 4

77. 5 × 1

78. 2 × 5

79. 4 × 5

80. 5 × 6

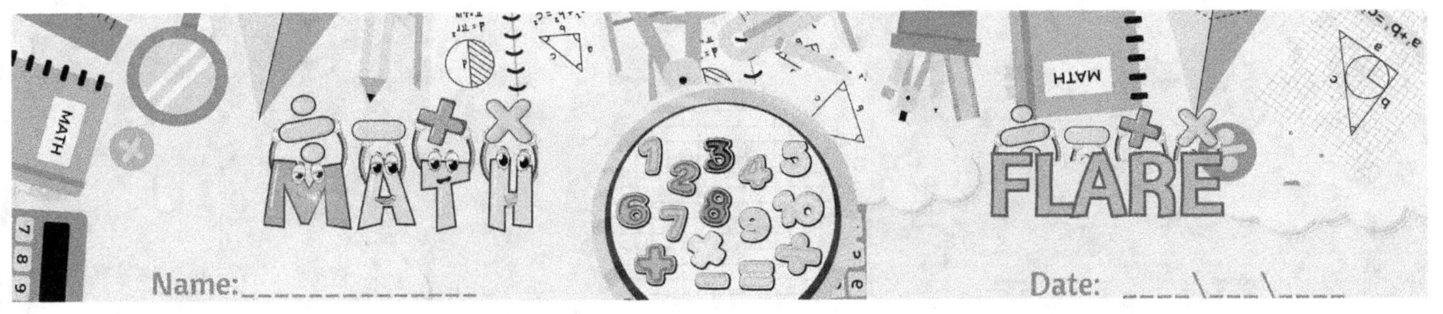

Multiplication by 6

81. $\begin{array}{r} 6 \\ \times\ 7 \\ \hline \end{array}$	82. $\begin{array}{r} 6 \\ \times\ 2 \\ \hline \end{array}$	83. $\begin{array}{r} 6 \\ \times\ 9 \\ \hline \end{array}$	84. $\begin{array}{r} 6 \\ \times\ 8 \\ \hline \end{array}$
85. $\begin{array}{r} 4 \\ \times\ 6 \\ \hline \end{array}$	86. $\begin{array}{r} 6 \\ \times\ 5 \\ \hline \end{array}$	87. $\begin{array}{r} 6 \\ \times\ 6 \\ \hline \end{array}$	88. $\begin{array}{r} 3 \\ \times\ 6 \\ \hline \end{array}$
89. $\begin{array}{r} 6 \\ \times\ 1 \\ \hline \end{array}$	90. $\begin{array}{r} 6 \\ \times\ 3 \\ \hline \end{array}$	91. $\begin{array}{r} 9 \\ \times\ 6 \\ \hline \end{array}$	92. $\begin{array}{r} 6 \\ \times\ 4 \\ \hline \end{array}$
93. $\begin{array}{r} 7 \\ \times\ 6 \\ \hline \end{array}$	94. $\begin{array}{r} 2 \\ \times\ 6 \\ \hline \end{array}$	95. $\begin{array}{r} 8 \\ \times\ 6 \\ \hline \end{array}$	96. $\begin{array}{r} 5 \\ \times\ 6 \\ \hline \end{array}$
97. $\begin{array}{r} 1 \\ \times\ 6 \\ \hline \end{array}$	98. $\begin{array}{r} 5 \\ \times\ 6 \\ \hline \end{array}$	99. $\begin{array}{r} 1 \\ \times\ 6 \\ \hline \end{array}$	100. $\begin{array}{r} 8 \\ \times\ 6 \\ \hline \end{array}$

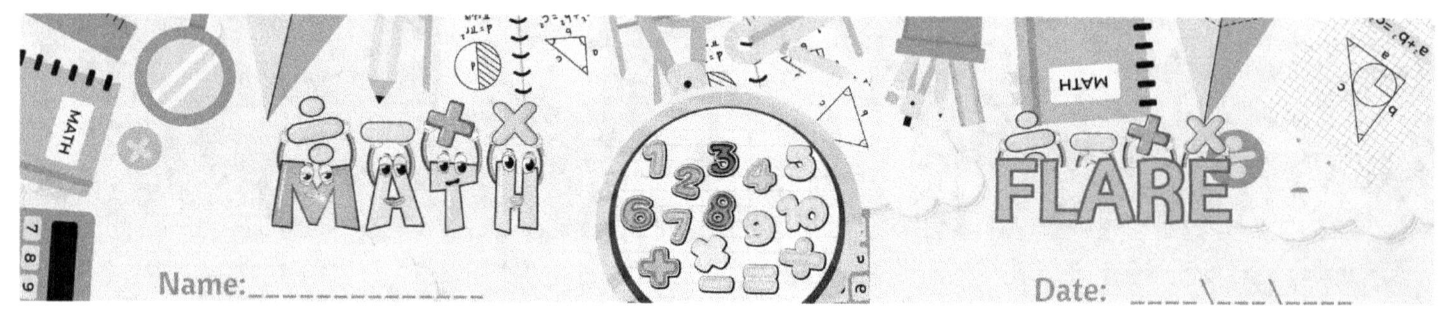

Multiplication by 7

101.
$$\begin{array}{r} 7 \\ \times\ 1 \\ \hline \end{array}$$

102.
$$\begin{array}{r} 7 \\ \times\ 7 \\ \hline \end{array}$$

103.
$$\begin{array}{r} 5 \\ \times\ 7 \\ \hline \end{array}$$

104.
$$\begin{array}{r} 7 \\ \times\ 3 \\ \hline \end{array}$$

105.
$$\begin{array}{r} 7 \\ \times\ 2 \\ \hline \end{array}$$

106.
$$\begin{array}{r} 7 \\ \times\ 6 \\ \hline \end{array}$$

107.
$$\begin{array}{r} 7 \\ \times\ 9 \\ \hline \end{array}$$

108.
$$\begin{array}{r} 4 \\ \times\ 7 \\ \hline \end{array}$$

109.
$$\begin{array}{r} 8 \\ \times\ 7 \\ \hline \end{array}$$

110.
$$\begin{array}{r} 3 \\ \times\ 7 \\ \hline \end{array}$$

111.
$$\begin{array}{r} 1 \\ \times\ 7 \\ \hline \end{array}$$

112.
$$\begin{array}{r} 7 \\ \times\ 5 \\ \hline \end{array}$$

113.
$$\begin{array}{r} 6 \\ \times\ 7 \\ \hline \end{array}$$

114.
$$\begin{array}{r} 7 \\ \times\ 8 \\ \hline \end{array}$$

115.
$$\begin{array}{r} 7 \\ \times\ 4 \\ \hline \end{array}$$

116.
$$\begin{array}{r} 9 \\ \times\ 7 \\ \hline \end{array}$$

117.
$$\begin{array}{r} 2 \\ \times\ 7 \\ \hline \end{array}$$

118.
$$\begin{array}{r} 8 \\ \times\ 7 \\ \hline \end{array}$$

119.
$$\begin{array}{r} 4 \\ \times\ 7 \\ \hline \end{array}$$

120.
$$\begin{array}{r} 7 \\ \times\ 1 \\ \hline \end{array}$$

Multiplication by 8

121.
  8
× 8

122.
  8
× 7

123.
  3
× 8

124.
  9
× 8

125.
  8
× 5

126.
  6
× 8

127.
  2
× 8

128.
  8
× 4

129.
  8
× 1

130.
  8
× 3

131.
  7
× 8

132.
  8
× 9

133.
  8
× 6

134.
  4
× 8

135.
  5
× 8

136.
  8
× 2

137.
  1
× 8

138.
  8
× 6

139.
  8
× 4

140.
  8
× 6

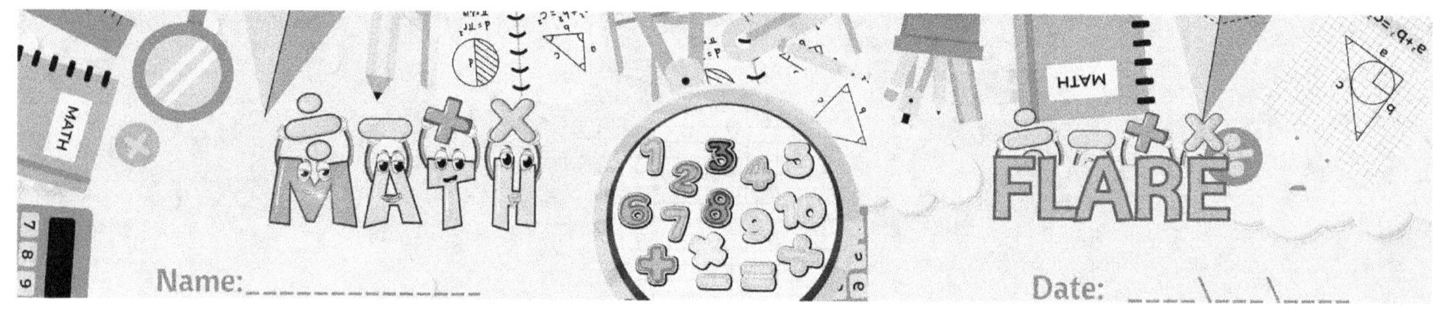

Multiplication by 9

141. $\begin{array}{r} 6 \\ \times\ 9 \\ \hline \end{array}$ 142. $\begin{array}{r} 9 \\ \times\ 7 \\ \hline \end{array}$ 143. $\begin{array}{r} 9 \\ \times\ 9 \\ \hline \end{array}$ 144. $\begin{array}{r} 9 \\ \times\ 2 \\ \hline \end{array}$

145. $\begin{array}{r} 9 \\ \times\ 3 \\ \hline \end{array}$ 146. $\begin{array}{r} 1 \\ \times\ 9 \\ \hline \end{array}$ 147. $\begin{array}{r} 9 \\ \times\ 5 \\ \hline \end{array}$ 148. $\begin{array}{r} 9 \\ \times\ 4 \\ \hline \end{array}$

149. $\begin{array}{r} 9 \\ \times\ 8 \\ \hline \end{array}$ 150. $\begin{array}{r} 7 \\ \times\ 9 \\ \hline \end{array}$ 151. $\begin{array}{r} 9 \\ \times\ 1 \\ \hline \end{array}$ 152. $\begin{array}{r} 4 \\ \times\ 9 \\ \hline \end{array}$

153. $\begin{array}{r} 5 \\ \times\ 9 \\ \hline \end{array}$ 154. $\begin{array}{r} 2 \\ \times\ 9 \\ \hline \end{array}$ 155. $\begin{array}{r} 8 \\ \times\ 9 \\ \hline \end{array}$ 156. $\begin{array}{r} 3 \\ \times\ 9 \\ \hline \end{array}$

157. $\begin{array}{r} 9 \\ \times\ 6 \\ \hline \end{array}$ 158. $\begin{array}{r} 5 \\ \times\ 9 \\ \hline \end{array}$ 159. $\begin{array}{r} 7 \\ \times\ 9 \\ \hline \end{array}$ 160. $\begin{array}{r} 9 \\ \times\ 8 \\ \hline \end{array}$

Multiplication by 10

161.   2
× 10

162.   10
× 4

163.   10
× 5

164.   6
× 10

165.   10
× 3

166.   9
× 10

167.   7
× 10

168.   8
× 10

169.   1
× 10

170.   10
× 6

171.   4
× 10

172.   10
× 2

173.   10
× 8

174.   10
× 7

175.   5
× 10

176.   10
× 1

177.   10
× 9

178.   3
× 10

179.   6
× 10

180.   10
× 3

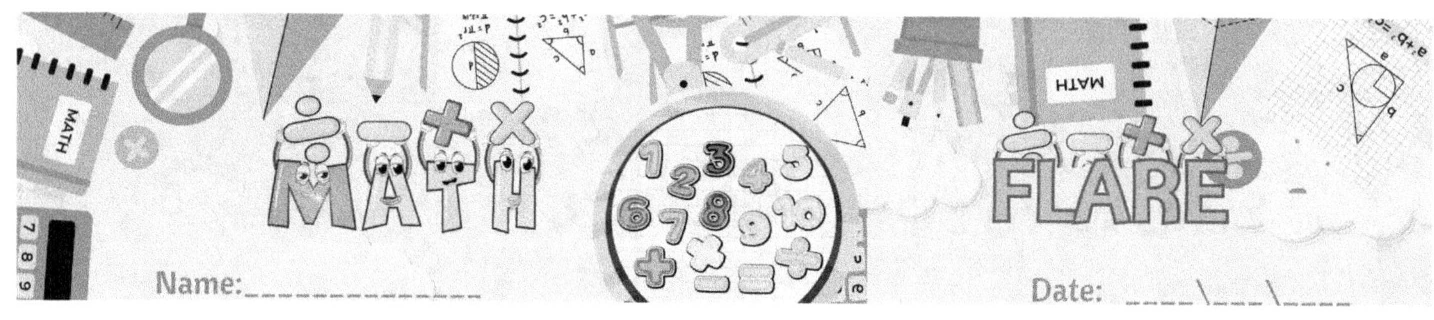

Basic Multiplication
Find the product.

181. 8 × 3	182. 3 × 5	183. 6 × 8	184. 8 × 7
185. 9 × 7	186. 7 × 9	187. 8 × 8	188. 4 × 4
189. 9 × 8	190. 8 × 1	191. 4 × 2	192. 5 × 7
193. 10 × 7	194. 10 × 2	195. 6 × 4	196. 5 × 9
197. 5 × 8	198. 1 × 6	199. 10 × 3	200. 2 × 5

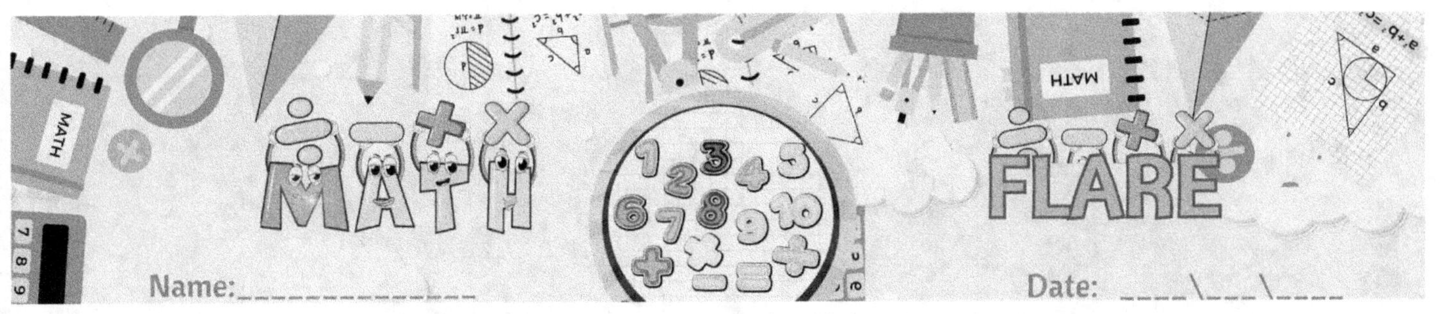

201. 4 × 3	202. 8 × 6	203. 4 × 8	204. 9 × 2
205. 10 × 9	206. 8 × 2	207. 7 × 8	208. 3 × 9
209. 5 × 2	210. 7 × 7	211. 3 × 4	212. 6 × 6
213. 4 × 10	214. 4 × 9	215. 6 × 7	216. 6 × 1
217. 6 × 9	218. 3 × 7	219. 7 × 3	220. 2 × 3

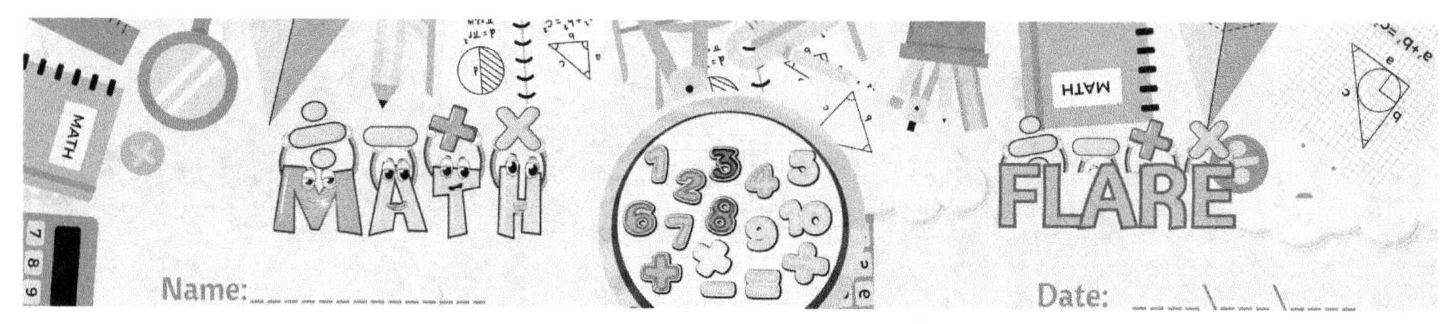

221.
$$\begin{array}{r} 8 \\ \times\ 9 \\ \hline \end{array}$$

222.
$$\begin{array}{r} 5 \\ \times\ 3 \\ \hline \end{array}$$

223.
$$\begin{array}{r} 3 \\ \times\ 6 \\ \hline \end{array}$$

224.
$$\begin{array}{r} 2 \\ \times\ 10 \\ \hline \end{array}$$

225.
$$\begin{array}{r} 1 \\ \times\ 3 \\ \hline \end{array}$$

226.
$$\begin{array}{r} 6 \\ \times\ 2 \\ \hline \end{array}$$

227.
$$\begin{array}{r} 3 \\ \times\ 8 \\ \hline \end{array}$$

228.
$$\begin{array}{r} 8 \\ \times\ 5 \\ \hline \end{array}$$

229.
$$\begin{array}{r} 2 \\ \times\ 2 \\ \hline \end{array}$$

230.
$$\begin{array}{r} 1 \\ \times\ 1 \\ \hline \end{array}$$

231.
$$\begin{array}{r} 1 \\ \times\ 5 \\ \hline \end{array}$$

232.
$$\begin{array}{r} 3 \\ \times\ 3 \\ \hline \end{array}$$

233.
$$\begin{array}{r} 2 \\ \times\ 7 \\ \hline \end{array}$$

234.
$$\begin{array}{r} 7 \\ \times\ 2 \\ \hline \end{array}$$

235.
$$\begin{array}{r} 7 \\ \times\ 10 \\ \hline \end{array}$$

236.
$$\begin{array}{r} 9 \\ \times\ 10 \\ \hline \end{array}$$

237.
$$\begin{array}{r} 4 \\ \times\ 6 \\ \hline \end{array}$$

238.
$$\begin{array}{r} 4 \\ \times\ 7 \\ \hline \end{array}$$

239.
$$\begin{array}{r} 5 \\ \times\ 1 \\ \hline \end{array}$$

240.
$$\begin{array}{r} 1 \\ \times\ 7 \\ \hline \end{array}$$

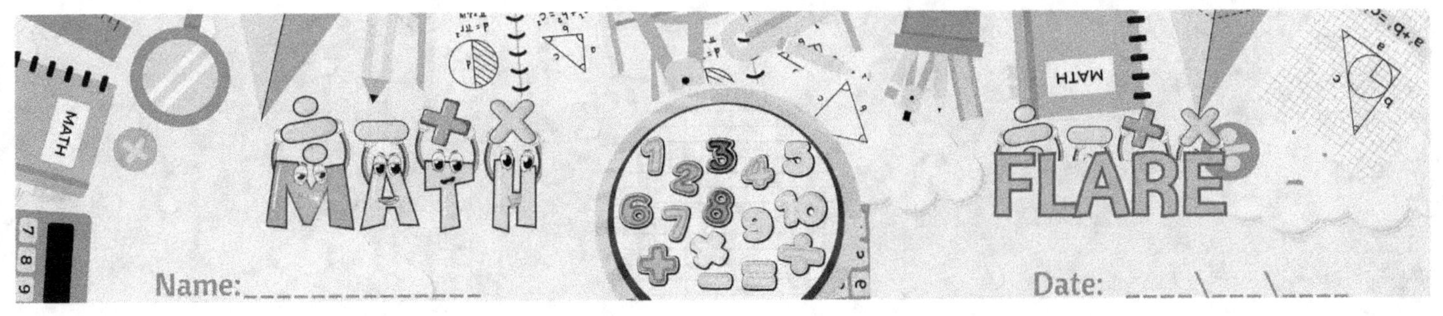

241. 2 × 4	242. 5 × 6	243. 7 × 5	244. 1 × 2
245. 6 × 5	246. 3 × 2	247. 2 × 8	248. 8 × 10
249. 7 × 6	250. 5 × 10	251. 10 × 8	252. 9 × 5
253. 10 × 6	254. 10 × 10	255. 4 × 5	256. 10 × 5
257. 1 × 4	258. 8 × 4	259. 1 × 8	260. 5 × 4

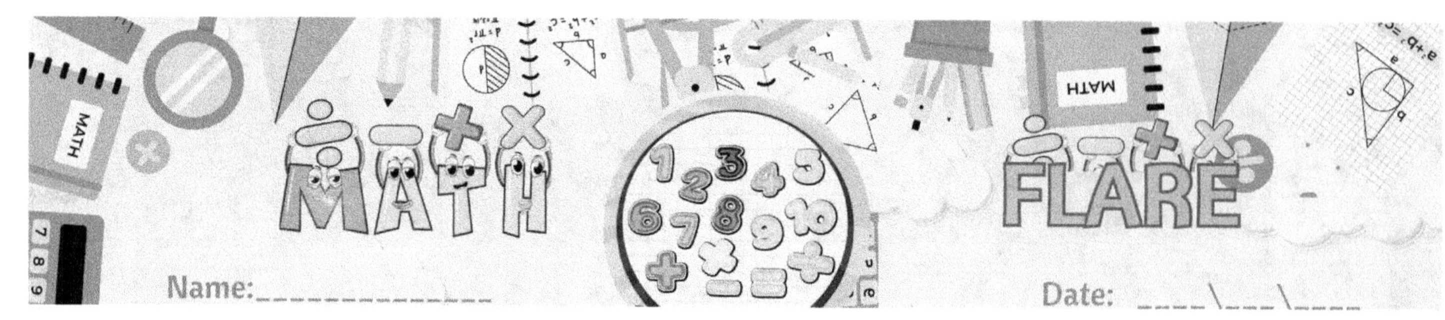

261. 7 × 4	262. 9 × 6	263. 2 × 6	264. 9 × 1
265. 9 × 9	266. 1 × 9	267. 9 × 4	268. 6 × 3
269. 2 × 1	270. 5 × 5	271. 7 × 1	272. 9 × 3
273. 4 × 1	274. 3 × 1	275. 2 × 9	276. 1 × 10
277. 10 × 1	278. 6 × 10	279. 3 × 10	280. 10 × 4

Multiplication: 2 x 1
Find the product.

281.   11
   × 4
	282. 41
	   × 2
		283. 31
		   × 2
			284. 10
			   × 4

285.   12
   × 4
	286. 11
	   × 3
		287. 22
		   × 4
			288. 21
			   × 3

289.   21
   × 4
	290. 22
	   × 2
		291. 34
		   × 2
			292. 20
			   × 2

293.   20
   × 3
	294. 32
	   × 3
		295. 12
		   × 2
			296. 88
			   × 1

297.   22
   × 3
	298. 40
	   × 2
		299. 33
		   × 3
			300. 10
			   × 2

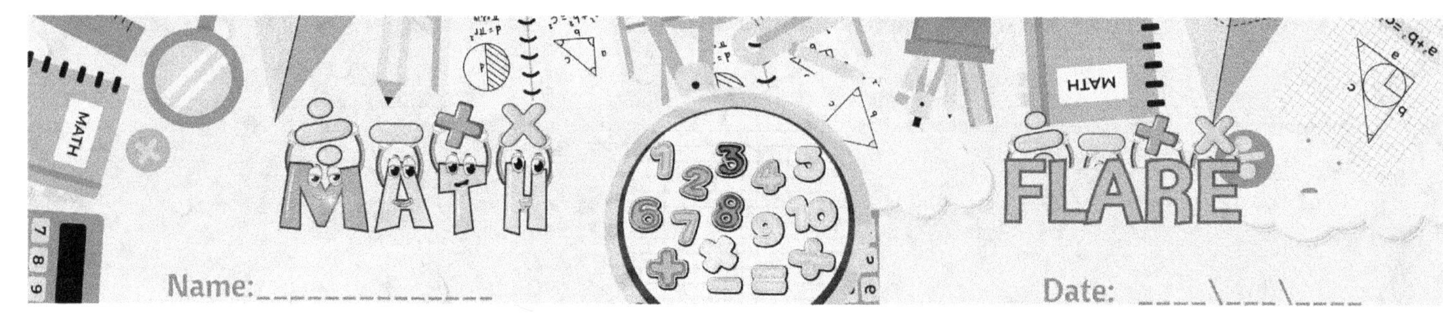

301. $\begin{array}{r} 86 \\ \times\ 1 \\ \hline \end{array}$	302. $\begin{array}{r} 32 \\ \times\ 2 \\ \hline \end{array}$	303. $\begin{array}{r} 43 \\ \times\ 2 \\ \hline \end{array}$	304. $\begin{array}{r} 75 \\ \times\ 1 \\ \hline \end{array}$
305. $\begin{array}{r} 30 \\ \times\ 3 \\ \hline \end{array}$	306. $\begin{array}{r} 49 \\ \times\ 1 \\ \hline \end{array}$	307. $\begin{array}{r} 10 \\ \times\ 5 \\ \hline \end{array}$	308. $\begin{array}{r} 20 \\ \times\ 4 \\ \hline \end{array}$
309. $\begin{array}{r} 11 \\ \times\ 5 \\ \hline \end{array}$	310. $\begin{array}{r} 38 \\ \times\ 1 \\ \hline \end{array}$	311. $\begin{array}{r} 89 \\ \times\ 1 \\ \hline \end{array}$	312. $\begin{array}{r} 30 \\ \times\ 2 \\ \hline \end{array}$
313. $\begin{array}{r} 80 \\ \times\ 1 \\ \hline \end{array}$	314. $\begin{array}{r} 13 \\ \times\ 2 \\ \hline \end{array}$	315. $\begin{array}{r} 27 \\ \times\ 1 \\ \hline \end{array}$	316. $\begin{array}{r} 31 \\ \times\ 3 \\ \hline \end{array}$
317. $\begin{array}{r} 10 \\ \times\ 3 \\ \hline \end{array}$	318. $\begin{array}{r} 42 \\ \times\ 2 \\ \hline \end{array}$	319. $\begin{array}{r} 47 \\ \times\ 1 \\ \hline \end{array}$	320. $\begin{array}{r} 11 \\ \times\ 2 \\ \hline \end{array}$

321.
$$\begin{array}{r} 12 \\ \times\ 3 \\ \hline \end{array}$$

322.
$$\begin{array}{r} 43 \\ \times\ 1 \\ \hline \end{array}$$

323.
$$\begin{array}{r} 35 \\ \times\ 1 \\ \hline \end{array}$$

324.
$$\begin{array}{r} 57 \\ \times\ 1 \\ \hline \end{array}$$

325.
$$\begin{array}{r} 98 \\ \times\ 1 \\ \hline \end{array}$$

326.
$$\begin{array}{r} 23 \\ \times\ 2 \\ \hline \end{array}$$

327.
$$\begin{array}{r} 71 \\ \times\ 1 \\ \hline \end{array}$$

328.
$$\begin{array}{r} 24 \\ \times\ 2 \\ \hline \end{array}$$

329.
$$\begin{array}{r} 33 \\ \times\ 2 \\ \hline \end{array}$$

330.
$$\begin{array}{r} 36 \\ \times\ 1 \\ \hline \end{array}$$

331.
$$\begin{array}{r} 39 \\ \times\ 1 \\ \hline \end{array}$$

332.
$$\begin{array}{r} 13 \\ \times\ 3 \\ \hline \end{array}$$

333.
$$\begin{array}{r} 95 \\ \times\ 1 \\ \hline \end{array}$$

334.
$$\begin{array}{r} 59 \\ \times\ 1 \\ \hline \end{array}$$

335.
$$\begin{array}{r} 23 \\ \times\ 3 \\ \hline \end{array}$$

336.
$$\begin{array}{r} 14 \\ \times\ 1 \\ \hline \end{array}$$

337.
$$\begin{array}{r} 21 \\ \times\ 2 \\ \hline \end{array}$$

338.
$$\begin{array}{r} 14 \\ \times\ 2 \\ \hline \end{array}$$

339.
$$\begin{array}{r} 93 \\ \times\ 1 \\ \hline \end{array}$$

340.
$$\begin{array}{r} 10 \\ \times\ 1 \\ \hline \end{array}$$

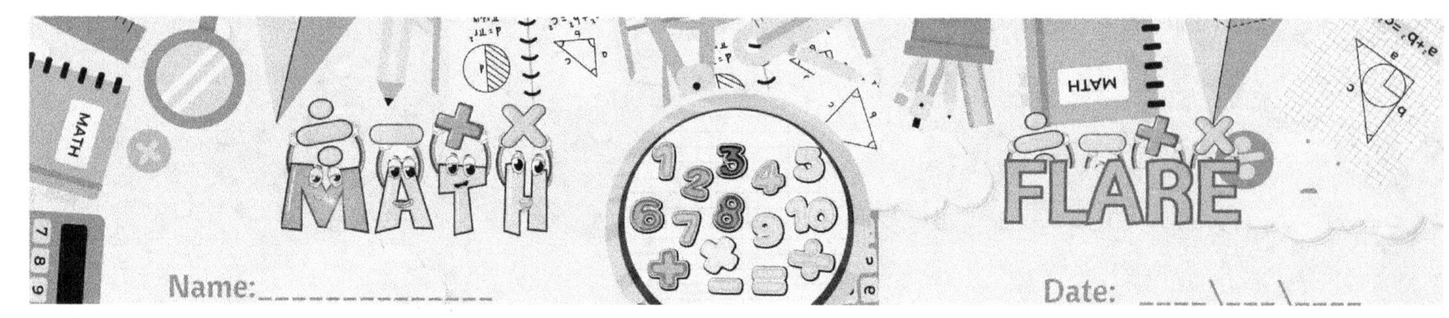

341. $\begin{array}{r} 44 \\ \times\ 2 \\ \hline \end{array}$	342. $\begin{array}{r} 20 \\ \times\ 1 \\ \hline \end{array}$	343. $\begin{array}{r} 90 \\ \times\ 1 \\ \hline \end{array}$	344. $\begin{array}{r} 97 \\ \times\ 1 \\ \hline \end{array}$
345. $\begin{array}{r} 52 \\ \times\ 1 \\ \hline \end{array}$	346. $\begin{array}{r} 94 \\ \times\ 1 \\ \hline \end{array}$	347. $\begin{array}{r} 48 \\ \times\ 1 \\ \hline \end{array}$	348. $\begin{array}{r} 72 \\ \times\ 1 \\ \hline \end{array}$
349. $\begin{array}{r} 81 \\ \times\ 1 \\ \hline \end{array}$	350. $\begin{array}{r} 58 \\ \times\ 1 \\ \hline \end{array}$	351. $\begin{array}{r} 29 \\ \times\ 1 \\ \hline \end{array}$	352. $\begin{array}{r} 30 \\ \times\ 1 \\ \hline \end{array}$
353. $\begin{array}{r} 73 \\ \times\ 1 \\ \hline \end{array}$	354. $\begin{array}{r} 77 \\ \times\ 1 \\ \hline \end{array}$	355. $\begin{array}{r} 42 \\ \times\ 1 \\ \hline \end{array}$	356. $\begin{array}{r} 51 \\ \times\ 1 \\ \hline \end{array}$
357. $\begin{array}{r} 74 \\ \times\ 1 \\ \hline \end{array}$	358. $\begin{array}{r} 31 \\ \times\ 1 \\ \hline \end{array}$	359. $\begin{array}{r} 92 \\ \times\ 1 \\ \hline \end{array}$	360. $\begin{array}{r} 61 \\ \times\ 1 \\ \hline \end{array}$

361. $\begin{array}{r} 84 \\ \times\ 1 \\ \hline \end{array}$	362. $\begin{array}{r} 68 \\ \times\ 1 \\ \hline \end{array}$	363. $\begin{array}{r} 50 \\ \times\ 1 \\ \hline \end{array}$	364. $\begin{array}{r} 99 \\ \times\ 1 \\ \hline \end{array}$
365. $\begin{array}{r} 21 \\ \times\ 1 \\ \hline \end{array}$	366. $\begin{array}{r} 62 \\ \times\ 1 \\ \hline \end{array}$	367. $\begin{array}{r} 54 \\ \times\ 1 \\ \hline \end{array}$	368. $\begin{array}{r} 37 \\ \times\ 1 \\ \hline \end{array}$
369. $\begin{array}{r} 76 \\ \times\ 1 \\ \hline \end{array}$	370. $\begin{array}{r} 78 \\ \times\ 1 \\ \hline \end{array}$	371. $\begin{array}{r} 32 \\ \times\ 1 \\ \hline \end{array}$	372. $\begin{array}{r} 34 \\ \times\ 1 \\ \hline \end{array}$
373. $\begin{array}{r} 45 \\ \times\ 1 \\ \hline \end{array}$	374. $\begin{array}{r} 15 \\ \times\ 1 \\ \hline \end{array}$	375. $\begin{array}{r} 16 \\ \times\ 1 \\ \hline \end{array}$	376. $\begin{array}{r} 28 \\ \times\ 1 \\ \hline \end{array}$
377. $\begin{array}{r} 41 \\ \times\ 1 \\ \hline \end{array}$	378. $\begin{array}{r} 23 \\ \times\ 1 \\ \hline \end{array}$	379. $\begin{array}{r} 63 \\ \times\ 1 \\ \hline \end{array}$	380. $\begin{array}{r} 91 \\ \times\ 1 \\ \hline \end{array}$

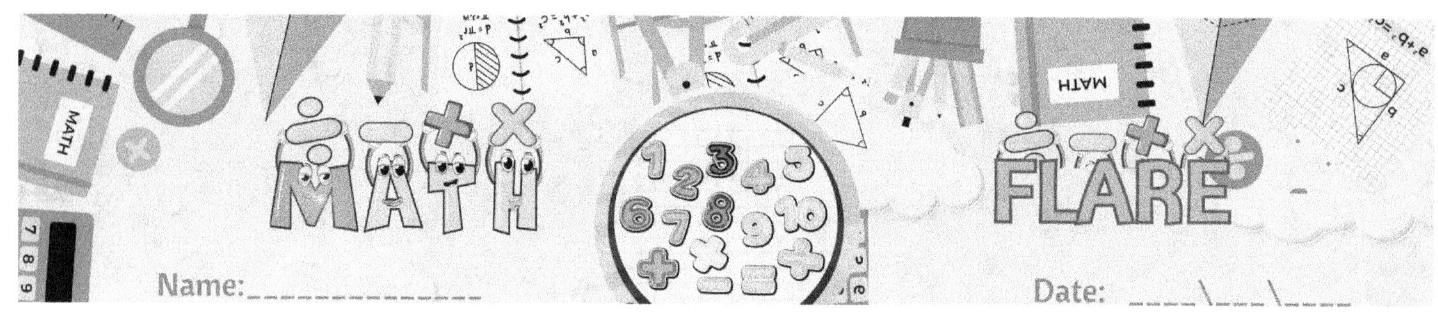

Multiplication: 3 x 1

Find the product.

381.
```
  202
×   4
-----
```

382.
```
  120
×   4
-----
```

383.
```
  223
×   3
-----
```

384.
```
  241
×   2
-----
```

385.
```
  333
×   2
-----
```

386.
```
  210
×   4
-----
```

387.
```
  242
×   2
-----
```

388.
```
  112
×   4
-----
```

389.
```
  311
×   2
-----
```

390.
```
  222
×   4
-----
```

391.
```
  938
×   1
-----
```

392.
```
  111
×   5
-----
```

393.
```
  231
×   3
-----
```

394.
```
  122
×   4
-----
```

395.
```
  812
×   1
-----
```

396.
```
  201
×   4
-----
```

397.
```
  344
×   2
-----
```

398.
```
  203
×   3
-----
```

399.
```
  404
×   2
-----
```

400.
```
  433
×   2
-----
```

401. 212 × 3	402. 200 × 4	403. 120 × 3	404. 101 × 5
405. 110 × 4	406. 212 × 4	407. 201 × 2	408. 304 × 2
409. 528 × 1	410. 430 × 2	411. 203 × 2	412. 332 × 3
413. 321 × 3	414. 222 × 3	415. 112 × 3	416. 123 × 3
417. 101 × 1	418. 330 × 3	419. 204 × 2	420. 140 × 2

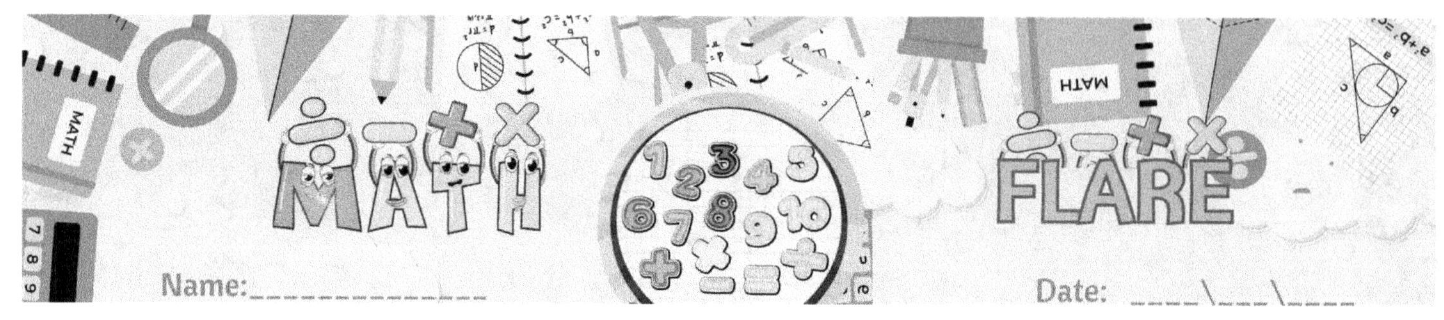

Name:___________________   Date: _______________

421. 111 × 3	422. 211 × 3	423. 100 × 4	424. 596 × 1
425. 334 × 2	426. 420 × 2	427. 945 × 1	428. 211 × 2
429. 101 × 4	430. 132 × 3	431. 110 × 5	432. 509 × 1
433. 130 × 3	434. 311 × 3	435. 333 × 3	436. 211 × 4
437. 213 × 3	438. 301 × 2	439. 153 × 1	440. 230 × 2

441.	233 × 2	442.	123 × 2	443.	330 × 2	444.	322 × 3
445.	100 × 3	446.	179 × 1	447.	343 × 2	448.	231 × 2
449.	413 × 2	450.	122 × 2	451.	104 × 2	452.	889 × 1
453.	113 × 3	454.	302 × 3	455.	337 × 1	456.	132 × 2
457.	102 × 2	458.	111 × 4	459.	320 × 3	460.	240 × 2

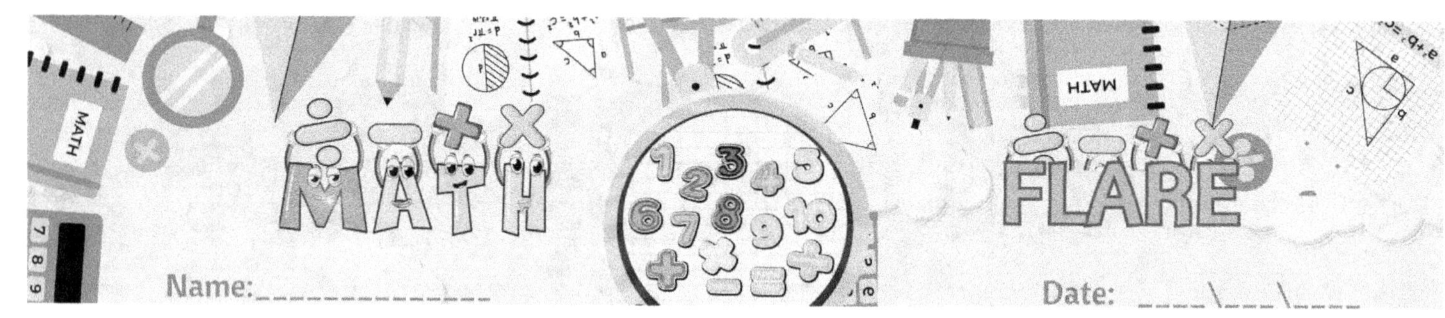

461. 100 × 5	462. 102 × 4	463. 202 × 2	464. 210 × 3
465. 221 × 4	466. 444 × 2	467. 648 × 1	468. 121 × 3
469. 121 × 4	470. 101 × 3	471. 401 × 2	472. 221 × 3
473. 617 × 1	474. 103 × 2	475. 129 × 1	476. 411 × 2
477. 442 × 2	478. 110 × 3	479. 310 × 3	480. 202 × 3

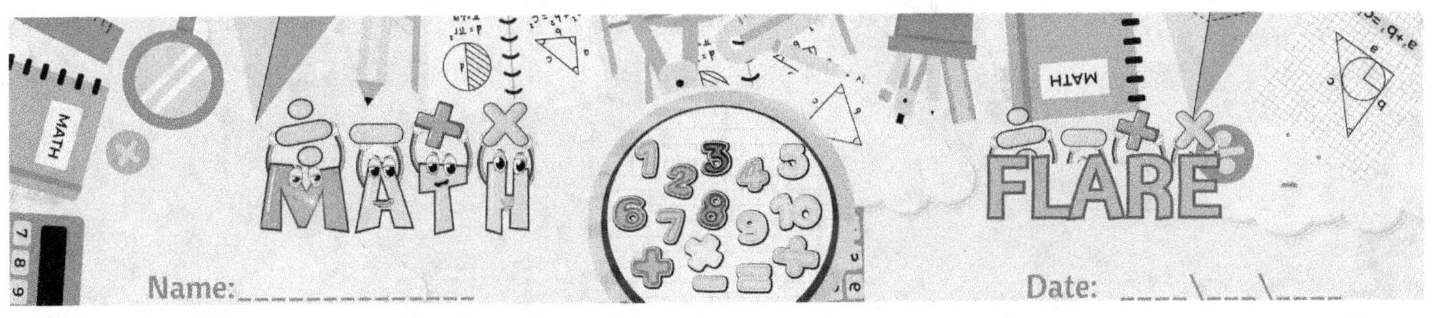

Commutative Property

Use the commutative property to fill the missing values.

481. 4 × __ = 2 × 4

482. 8 × 5 = 5 × __

483. 6 × __ = 9 × 6

484. __ × 2 = 2 × 5

485. 8 × __ = 9 × 8

486. 9 × 7 = 7 × __

487. 9 × 5 = __ × 9

488. 7 × __ = 10 × 7

489. 8 × 4 = __ × 8

490. __ × 8 = 8 × 4

491. 1 × 3 = __ × 1

492. 7 × __ = 8 × 7

493. 2 × 4 = __ × 2

494. __ × 5 = 5 × 10

495. 8 × 2 = 2 × __

496. 10 × __ = 3 × 10

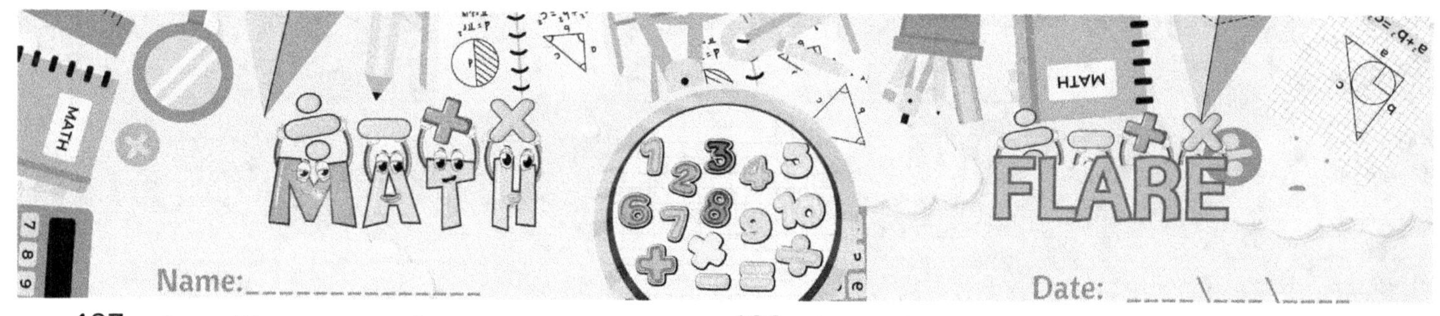

497. 4 × 7 = __ × 4

498. 1 × 7 = 7 × __

499. 4 × 3 = __ × 4

500. 6 × __ = 8 × 6

501. 7 × 6 = 6 × __

502. 10 × 4 = 4 × __

503. 9 × 2 = 2 × __

504. 8 × 3 = 3 × __

505. 3 × __ = 1 × 3

506. 2 × __ = 3 × 2

507. 2 × 7 = 7 × __

508. 8 × 10 = __ × 8

509. 4 × 10 = __ × 4

510. __ × 9 = 9 × 3

511. 2 × __ = 10 × 2

512. 6 × 10 = 10 × __

513. __ × 1 = 1 × 9

514. 5 × 1 = 1 × __

515. ___ × 9 = 9 × 10

516. ___ × 9 = 9 × 7

517. 1 × 6 = 6 × __

518. 4 × 9 = 9 × __

519. 3 × __ = 8 × 3

520. 5 × 7 = 7 × __

521. 4 × __ = 6 × 4

522. 8 × 7 = __ × 8

523. 3 × 2 = __ × 3

524. 1 × 8 = __ × 1

525. 2 × __ = 6 × 2

526. __ × 3 = 3 × 9

527. 3 × 5 = __ × 3

528. 5 × 9 = 9 × __

529. __ × 7 = 7 × 3

530. 9 × __ = 8 × 9

531. 2 × 9 = __ × 2

532. 7 × 5 = 5 × __

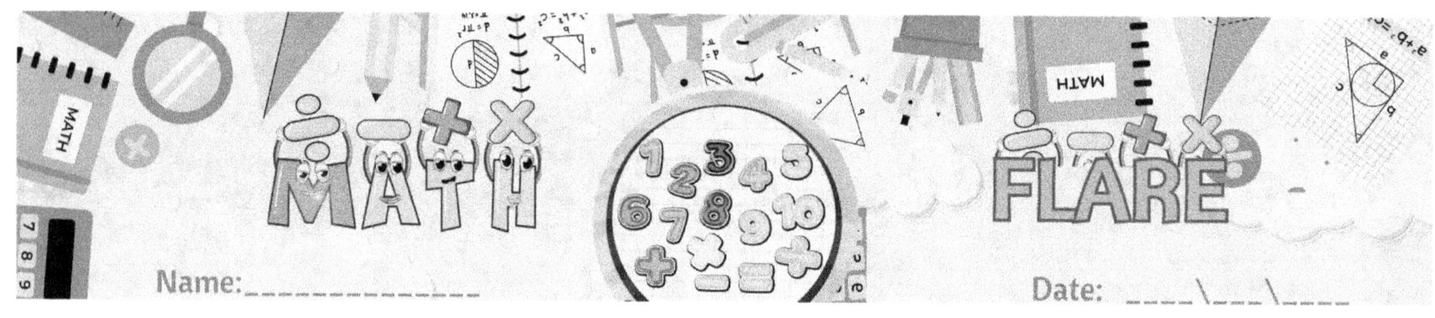

Division by 2

Find the quotient.

533.
$2\overline{)8}$

534.
$2\overline{)32}$

535.
$2\overline{)6}$

536.
$2\overline{)18}$

537.
$2\overline{)22}$

538.
$2\overline{)14}$

539.
$2\overline{)36}$

540.
$2\overline{)4}$

541.
$2\overline{)10}$

542.
$2\overline{)26}$

543.
$2\overline{)2}$

544.
$2\overline{)30}$

545.
$2\overline{)24}$

546.
$2\overline{)16}$

547.
$2\overline{)20}$

548.
$2\overline{)34}$

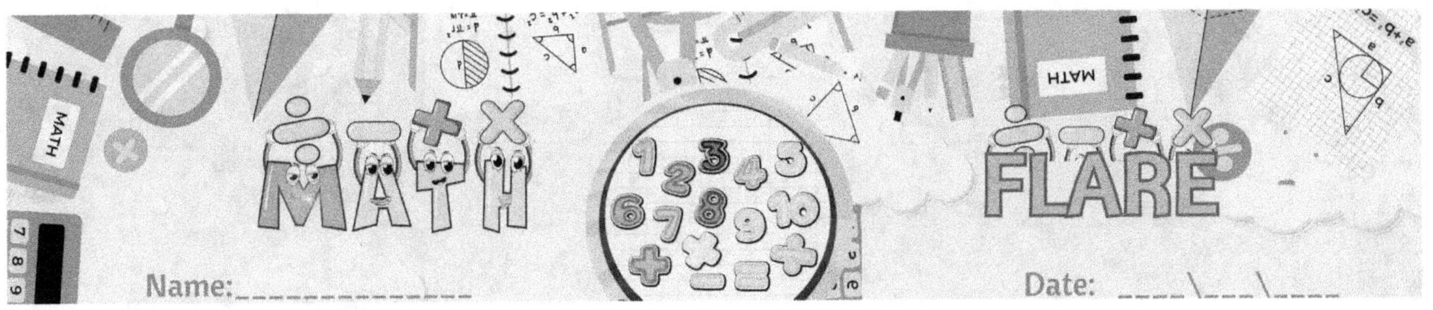

Division by 3

Find the quotient.

549. 3)24

550. 3)18

551. 3)9

552. 3)33

553. 3)15

554. 3)45

555. 3)39

556. 3)36

557. 3)6

558. 3)12

559. 3)21

560. 3)51

561. 3)42

562. 3)27

563. 3)30

564. 3)54

565. 3)48

566. 3)57

567. 3)60

568. 3)3

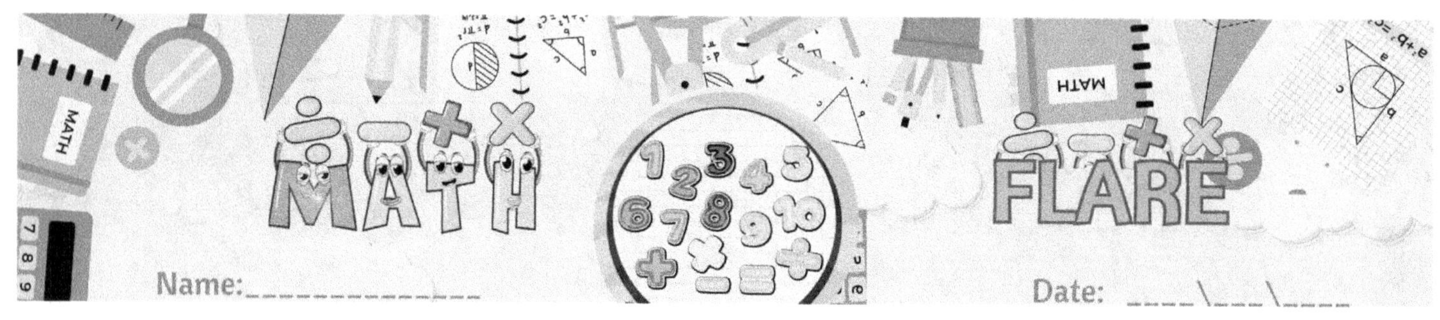

Division by 4

Find the quotient.

569.
$4\overline{)32}$

570.
$4\overline{)20}$

571.
$4\overline{)76}$

572.
$4\overline{)56}$

573.
$4\overline{)64}$

574.
$4\overline{)16}$

575.
$4\overline{)72}$

576.
$4\overline{)4}$

577.
$4\overline{)60}$

578.
$4\overline{)24}$

579.
$4\overline{)28}$

580.
$4\overline{)44}$

581.
$4\overline{)36}$

582.
$4\overline{)80}$

583.
$4\overline{)12}$

584.
$4\overline{)52}$

585.
$4\overline{)68}$

586.
$4\overline{)40}$

587.
$4\overline{)8}$

588.
$4\overline{)48}$

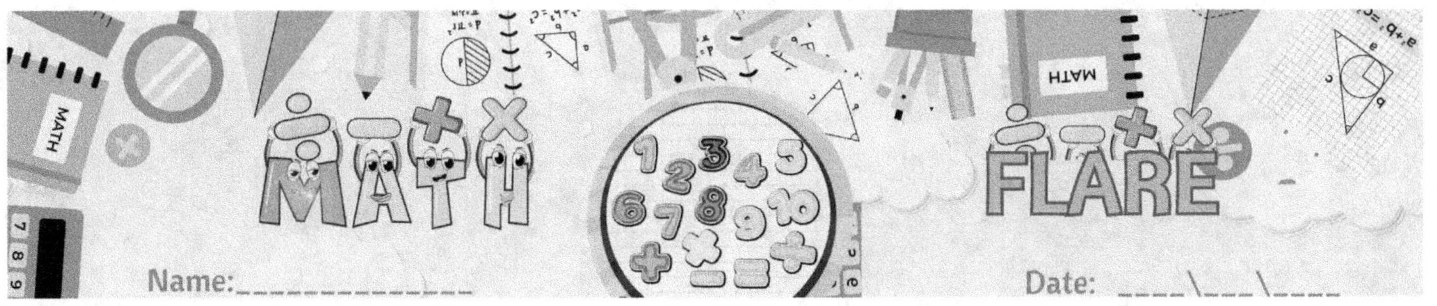

Division by 5

Find the quotient.

589.

$5\overline{)85}$

590.

$5\overline{)15}$

591.

$5\overline{)55}$

592.

$5\overline{)5}$

593.

$5\overline{)35}$

594.

$5\overline{)90}$

595.

$5\overline{)25}$

596.

$5\overline{)65}$

597.

$5\overline{)60}$

598.

$5\overline{)10}$

599.

$5\overline{)70}$

600.

$5\overline{)30}$

601.

$5\overline{)100}$

602.

$5\overline{)50}$

603.

$5\overline{)75}$

604.

$5\overline{)95}$

605.

$5\overline{)45}$

606.

$5\overline{)20}$

607.

$5\overline{)80}$

608.

$5\overline{)40}$

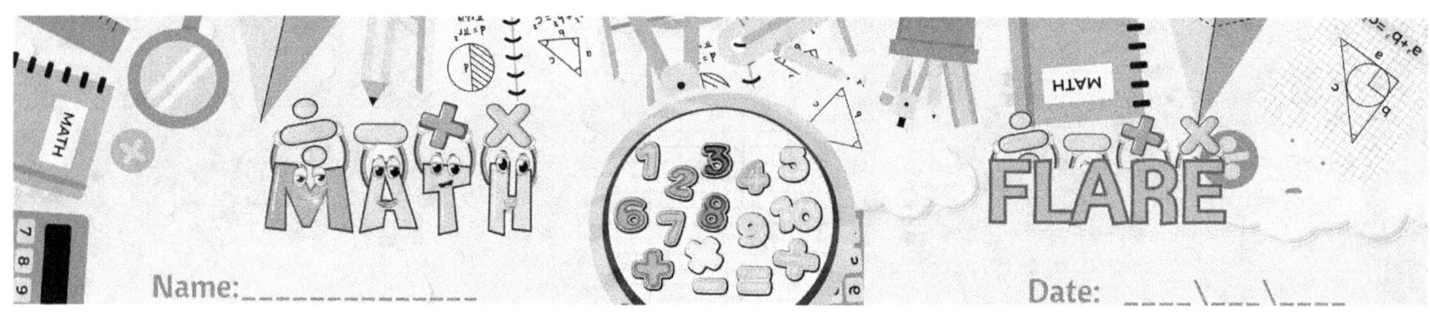

Division by 6

Find the quotient.

609. $6\overline{)72}$

610. $6\overline{)18}$

611. $6\overline{)42}$

612. $6\overline{)36}$

613. $6\overline{)90}$

614. $6\overline{)24}$

615. $6\overline{)96}$

616. $6\overline{)12}$

617. $6\overline{)6}$

618. $6\overline{)66}$

619. $6\overline{)48}$

620. $6\overline{)102}$

621. $6\overline{)60}$

622. $6\overline{)84}$

623. $6\overline{)78}$

624. $6\overline{)114}$

625. $6\overline{)54}$

626. $6\overline{)30}$

627. $6\overline{)108}$

628. $6\overline{)120}$

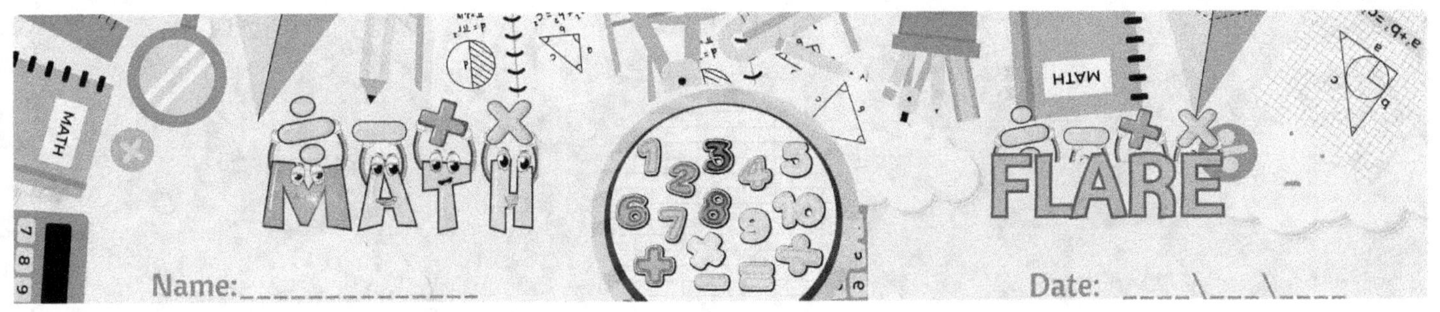

Division by 7

Find the quotient.

629. $7\overline{)28}$

630. $7\overline{)56}$

631. $7\overline{)21}$

632. $7\overline{)84}$

633. $7\overline{)70}$

634. $7\overline{)42}$

635. $7\overline{)91}$

636. $7\overline{)126}$

637. $7\overline{)133}$

638. $7\overline{)14}$

639. $7\overline{)140}$

640. $7\overline{)119}$

641. $7\overline{)112}$

642. $7\overline{)49}$

643. $7\overline{)35}$

644. $7\overline{)105}$

645. $7\overline{)77}$

646. $7\overline{)7}$

647. $7\overline{)63}$

648. $7\overline{)98}$

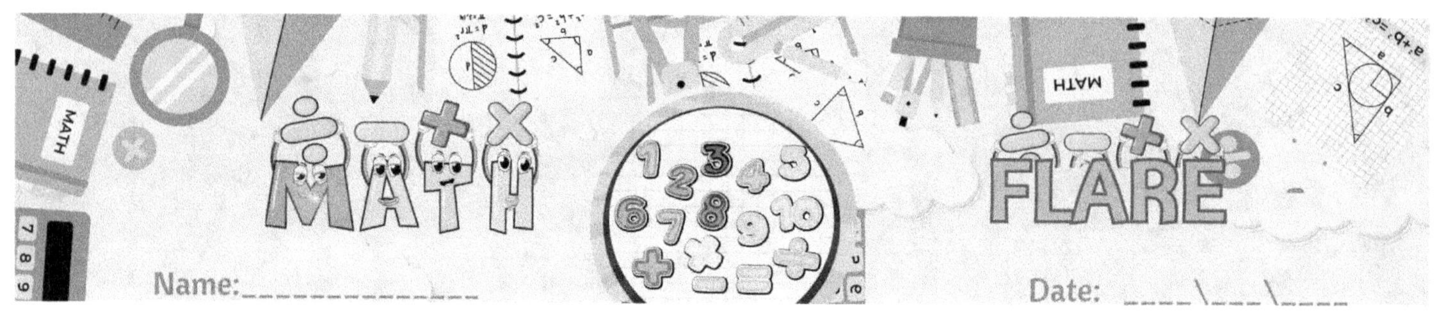

Division by 8

Find the quotient.

649. $8\overline{)40}$	650. $8\overline{)96}$	651. $8\overline{)80}$	652. $8\overline{)64}$
653. $8\overline{)112}$	654. $8\overline{)48}$	655. $8\overline{)32}$	656. $8\overline{)16}$
657. $8\overline{)144}$	658. $8\overline{)152}$	659. $8\overline{)120}$	660. $8\overline{)88}$
661. $8\overline{)128}$	662. $8\overline{)56}$	663. $8\overline{)8}$	664. $8\overline{)104}$
665. $8\overline{)72}$	666. $8\overline{)136}$	667. $8\overline{)24}$	668. $8\overline{)160}$

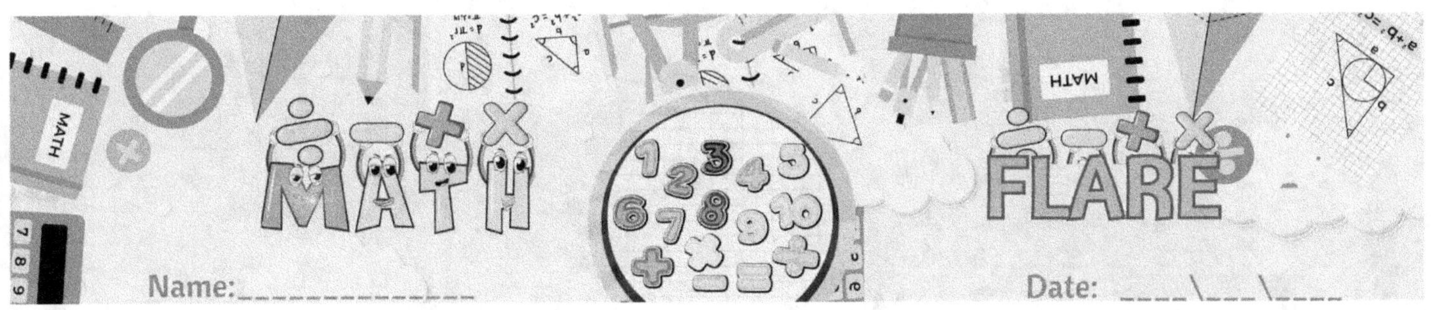

Division by 9

Find the quotient.

669.
$$9\overline{)36}$$

670.
$$9\overline{)54}$$

671.
$$9\overline{)126}$$

672.
$$9\overline{)144}$$

673.
$$9\overline{)45}$$

674.
$$9\overline{)81}$$

675.
$$9\overline{)99}$$

676.
$$9\overline{)18}$$

677.
$$9\overline{)162}$$

678.
$$9\overline{)63}$$

679.
$$9\overline{)9}$$

680.
$$9\overline{)90}$$

681.
$$9\overline{)27}$$

682.
$$9\overline{)72}$$

683.
$$9\overline{)180}$$

684.
$$9\overline{)153}$$

685.
$$9\overline{)171}$$

686.
$$9\overline{)108}$$

687.
$$9\overline{)117}$$

688.
$$9\overline{)135}$$

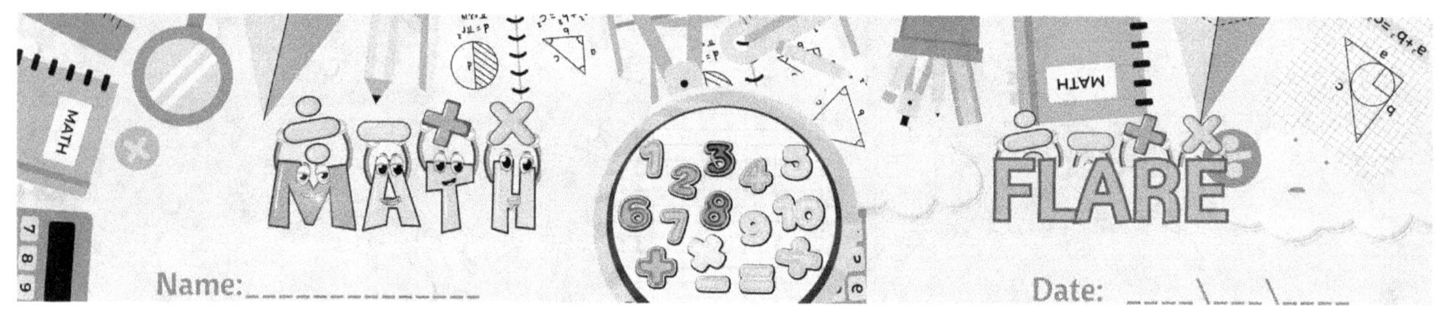

Division by 10

Find the quotient.

689.

$10 \overline{)10}$

690.

$10 \overline{)30}$

691.

$10 \overline{)90}$

692.

$10 \overline{)20}$

693.

$10 \overline{)150}$

694.

$10 \overline{)170}$

695.

$10 \overline{)100}$

696.

$10 \overline{)80}$

697.

$10 \overline{)70}$

698.

$10 \overline{)50}$

699.

$10 \overline{)130}$

700.

$10 \overline{)160}$

701.

$10 \overline{)120}$

702.

$10 \overline{)140}$

703.

$10 \overline{)190}$

Basic Division

Find the quotient.

704. $8\overline{)152}$	705. $9\overline{)81}$	706. $2\overline{)32}$	707. $8\overline{)72}$
708. $9\overline{)153}$	709. $7\overline{)84}$	710. $3\overline{)60}$	711. $5\overline{)10}$
712. $9\overline{)162}$	713. $3\overline{)18}$	714. $2\overline{)8}$	715. $9\overline{)27}$
716. $9\overline{)54}$	717. $6\overline{)18}$	718. $7\overline{)49}$	719. $7\overline{)119}$
720. $10\overline{)80}$	721. $8\overline{)24}$	722. $1\overline{)13}$	723. $2\overline{)30}$

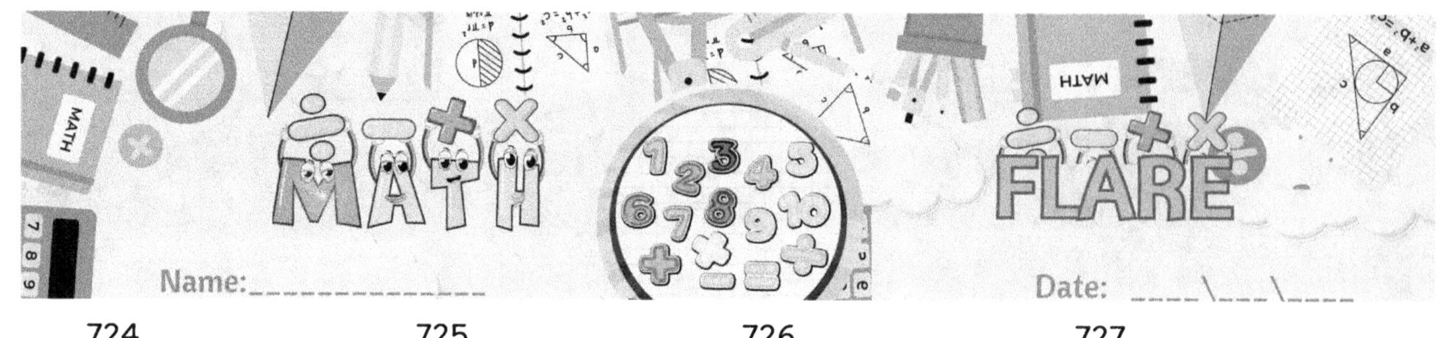

Name:________________   Date: ____________

724.

2)24

725.

7)21

726.

7)105

727.

5)90

728.

8)96

729.

1)15

730.

10)30

731.

9)90

732.

9)135

733.

9)171

734.

4)52

735.

2)20

736.

3)12

737.

4)68

738.

2)14

739.

10)140

740.

10)60

741.

7)70

742.

5)25

743.

5)85

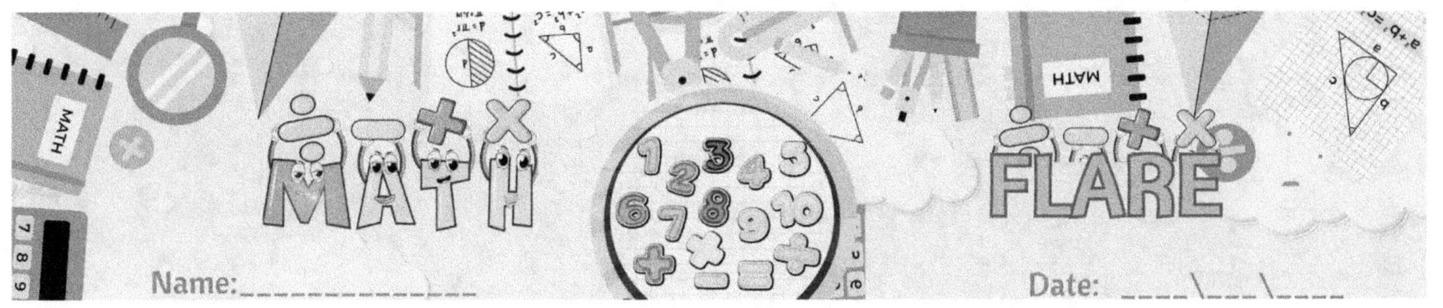

744.

$8\overline{)32}$

745.

$3\overline{)27}$

746.

$5\overline{)30}$

747.

$9\overline{)36}$

748.

$4\overline{)80}$

749.

$10\overline{)40}$

750.

$6\overline{)42}$

751.

$6\overline{)114}$

752.

$5\overline{)75}$

753.

$8\overline{)56}$

754.

$2\overline{)28}$

755.

$9\overline{)72}$

756.

$3\overline{)42}$

757.

$4\overline{)8}$

758.

$2\overline{)22}$

759.

$10\overline{)180}$

760.

$6\overline{)84}$

761.

$8\overline{)128}$

762.

$9\overline{)117}$

763.

$5\overline{)35}$

764.

$7\overline{)28}$

765.

$3\overline{)33}$

766.

$7\overline{)7}$

767.

$6\overline{)60}$

768.

$6\overline{)12}$

769.

$10\overline{)10}$

770.

$9\overline{)144}$

771.

$2\overline{)4}$

772.

$4\overline{)56}$

773.

$6\overline{)72}$

774.

$3\overline{)9}$

775.

$8\overline{)40}$

776.

$2\overline{)12}$

777.

$8\overline{)144}$

778.

$6\overline{)102}$

779.

$6\overline{)6}$

780.

$1\overline{)10}$

781.

$4\overline{)28}$

782.

$9\overline{)108}$

783.

$8\overline{)16}$

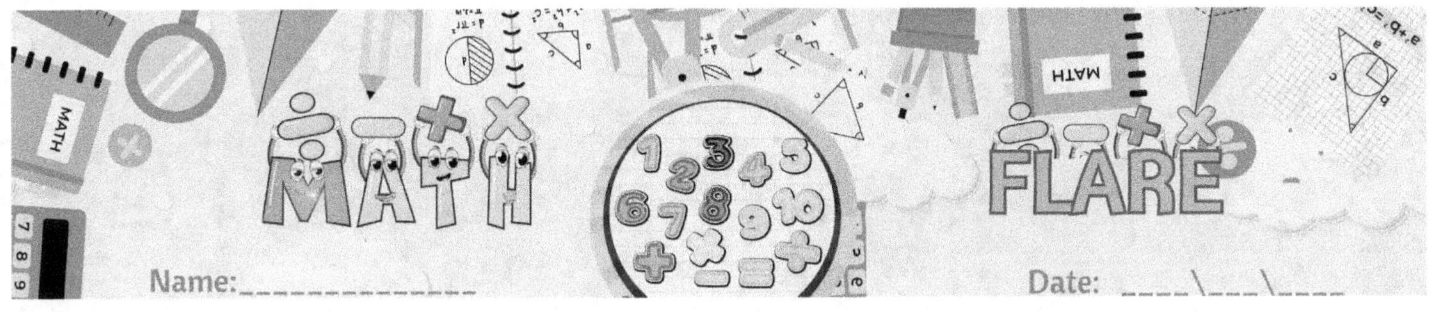

784. 6)54	785. 3)36	786. 10)20	787. 6)30
788. 8)64	789. 9)126	790. 10)170	791. 6)36
792. 1)17	793. 4)24	794. 4)40	795. 3)57
796. 1)6	797. 5)80	798. 3)51	799. 7)14
800. 2)10	801. 9)45	802. 6)120	803. 3)45

804.
$$10\overline{)160}$$

805.
$$7\overline{)91}$$

806.
$$4\overline{)36}$$

807.
$$3\overline{)15}$$

808.
$$2\overline{)18}$$

809.
$$1\overline{)18}$$

810.
$$9\overline{)63}$$

811.
$$8\overline{)80}$$

812.
$$10\overline{)100}$$

813.
$$9\overline{)180}$$

814.
$$4\overline{)44}$$

815.
$$7\overline{)63}$$

816.
$$4\overline{)48}$$

817.
$$1\overline{)4}$$

818.
$$2\overline{)36}$$

819.
$$7\overline{)112}$$

820.
$$5\overline{)70}$$

821.
$$8\overline{)104}$$

822.
$$5\overline{)60}$$

823.
$$8\overline{)160}$$

824. $10\overline{)130}$	**825.** $2\overline{)16}$	**826.** $7\overline{)42}$	**827.** $4\overline{)20}$
828. $1\overline{)1}$	**829.** $2\overline{)38}$	**830.** $2\overline{)34}$	**831.** $10\overline{)90}$
832. $8\overline{)112}$	**833.** $5\overline{)20}$	**834.** $2\overline{)6}$	**835.** $2\overline{)26}$
836. $7\overline{)77}$	**837.** $4\overline{)76}$	**838.** $5\overline{)15}$	**839.** $10\overline{)200}$
840. $3\overline{)39}$	**841.** $5\overline{)95}$	**842.** $7\overline{)140}$	**843.** $6\overline{)66}$

844. $1 \overline{)8}$

845. $7 \overline{)133}$

846. $1 \overline{)2}$

847. $7 \overline{)98}$

848. $5 \overline{)55}$

849. $5 \overline{)45}$

850. $6 \overline{)90}$

851. $4 \overline{)16}$

852. $8 \overline{)136}$

853. $6 \overline{)108}$

854. $8 \overline{)120}$

855. $4 \overline{)64}$

856. $1 \overline{)11}$

857. $2 \overline{)40}$

858. $6 \overline{)78}$

859. $4 \overline{)4}$

860. $7 \overline{)35}$

861. $7 \overline{)56}$

862. $10 \overline{)120}$

863. $10 \overline{)150}$

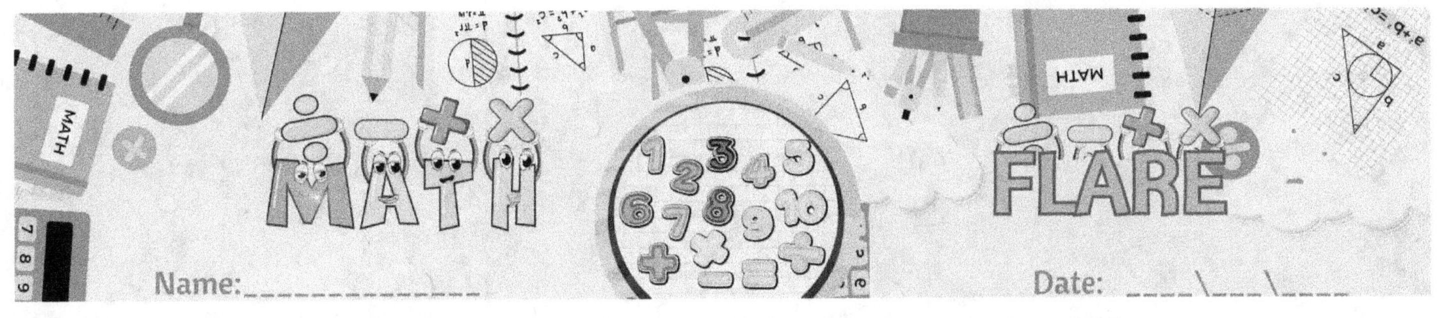

864. $5\overline{)65}$	865. $6\overline{)96}$	866. $7\overline{)126}$	867. $10\overline{)110}$
868. $4\overline{)60}$	869. $4\overline{)12}$	870. $3\overline{)48}$	871. $5\overline{)40}$
872. $1\overline{)3}$	873. $3\overline{)54}$	874. $9\overline{)18}$	875. $5\overline{)100}$
876. $3\overline{)30}$	877. $9\overline{)9}$	878. $8\overline{)88}$	879. $3\overline{)6}$
880. $5\overline{)50}$	881. $4\overline{)72}$	882. $1\overline{)19}$	883. $3\overline{)21}$

884. $1\overline{)14}$

885. $3\overline{)24}$

886. $6\overline{)24}$

887. $10\overline{)50}$

888. $6\overline{)48}$

889. $1\overline{)16}$

890. $5\overline{)5}$

891. $4\overline{)32}$

892. $9\overline{)99}$

893. $3\overline{)3}$

894. $1\overline{)5}$

895. $2\overline{)2}$

896. $8\overline{)48}$

897. $1\overline{)12}$

898. $1\overline{)9}$

899. $8\overline{)8}$

900. $10\overline{)190}$

901. $1\overline{)20}$

902. $1\overline{)7}$

903. $10\overline{)70}$

Matching the answers.

904.

a. $16 \div 4 =$ _______ •   • J = 8

b. $1 \times 2 =$ _______ •   • G = 5

c. $1 \times 9 =$ _______ •   • A = 1

d. $54 \div 6 =$ _______ •   • I = 21

e. $1 \times 5 =$ _______ •   • F = 4

f. $8 \times 1 =$ _______ •   • E = 9

g. $7 \times 6 =$ _______ •   • H = 8

h. $2 \times 4 =$ _______ •   • B = 42

i. $7 \times 3 =$ _______ •   • C = 9

j. $4 \div 4 =$ _______ •   • D = 2

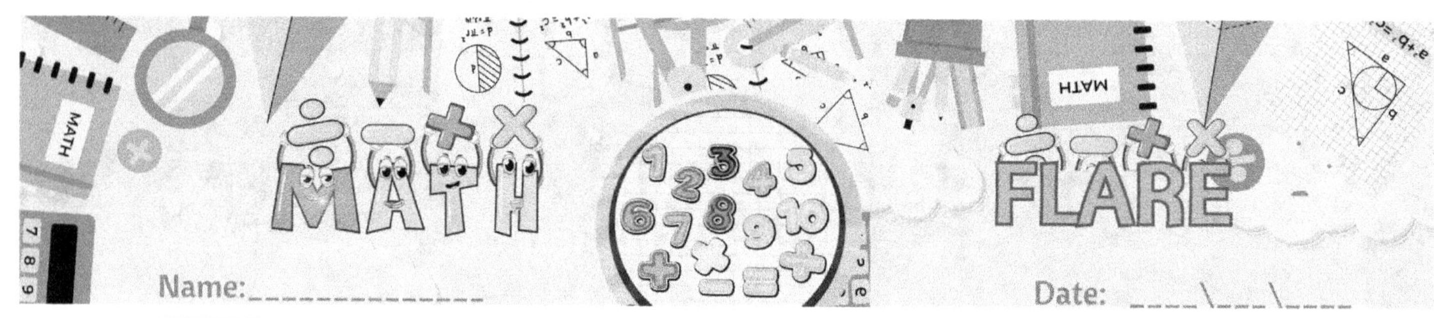

905.

a. 8 ÷ 8 = _______ •

b. 4 ÷ 1 = _______ •

c. 10 × 10 = _______ •

d. 70 ÷ 7 = _______ •

e. 3 × 2 = _______ •

f. 30 ÷ 3 = _______ •

g. 56 ÷ 7 = _______ •

h. 27 ÷ 3 = _______ •

i. 7 × 2 = _______ •

j. 40 ÷ 4 = _______ •

• C = 10

• G = 14

• I = 100

• H = 4

• E = 10

• J = 10

• D = 6

• A = 8

• F = 9

• B = 1

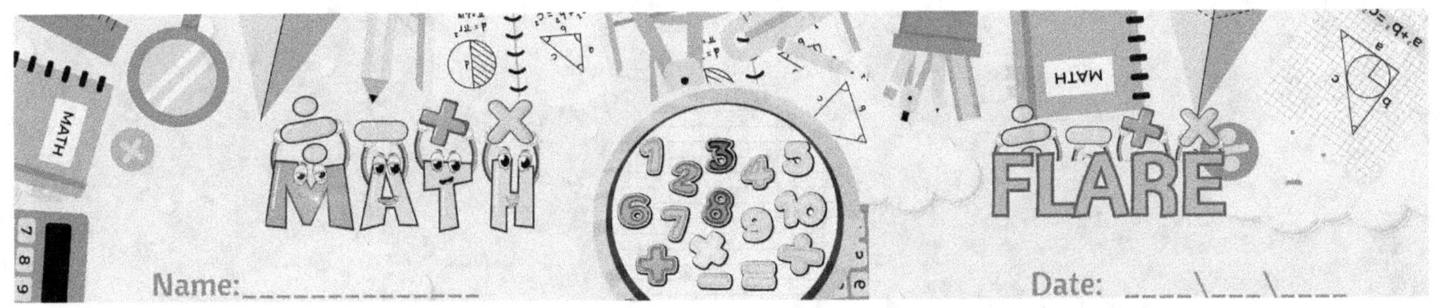

906.

a. $40 \div 10 =$ ______ •	• F = 4
b. $56 \div 8 =$ ______ •	• B = 42
c. $32 \div 8 =$ ______ •	• J = 40
d. $8 \times 8 =$ ______ •	• C = 12
e. $6 \times 7 =$ ______ •	• A = 4
f. $30 \div 10 =$ ______ •	• G = 4
g. $3 \times 4 =$ ______ •	• H = 7
h. $12 \div 3 =$ ______ •	• D = 3
i. $5 \times 8 =$ ______ •	• I = 64
j. $4 \div 1 =$ ______ •	• E = 4

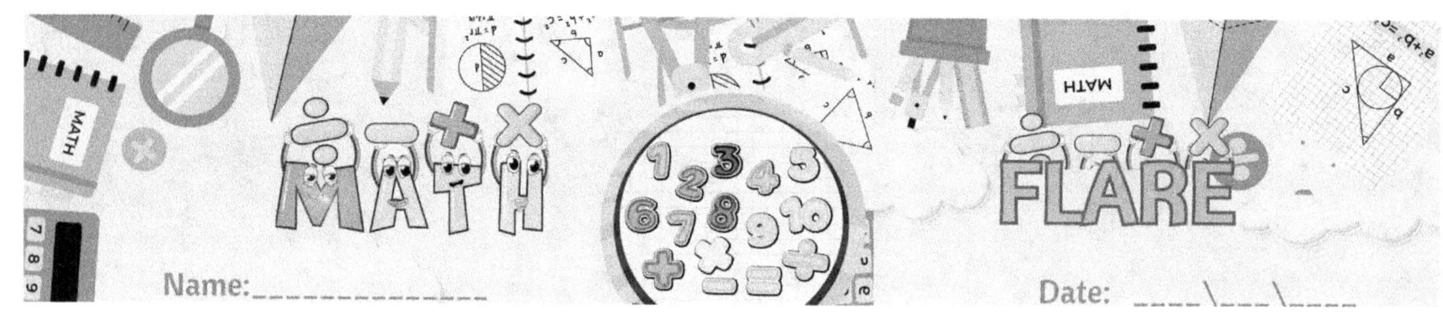

907.

a. 49 ÷ 7 = _______ •	• A = 6
b. 42 ÷ 7 = _______ •	• I = 16
c. 9 × 7 = _______ •	• E = 3
d. 3 × 1 = _______ •	• G = 7
e. 18 ÷ 3 = _______ •	• H = 6
f. 15 ÷ 5 = _______ •	• B = 63
g. 8 × 2 = _______ •	• F = 9
h. 18 ÷ 2 = _______ •	• C = 3
i. 27 ÷ 3 = _______ •	• J = 4
j. 36 ÷ 9 = _______ •	• D = 9

908.

a. 20 ÷ 4 = _______ •

b. 45 ÷ 9 = _______ •

c. 4 × 7 = _______ •

d. 9 × 9 = _______ •

e. 6 × 10 = _______ •

f. 9 × 8 = _______ •

g. 27 ÷ 3 = _______ •

h. 8 × 7 = _______ •

i. 9 ÷ 9 = _______ •

j. 10 × 8 = _______ •

• H = 60

• D = 81

• B = 56

• F = 1

• E = 9

• J = 5

• C = 72

• G = 28

• A = 5

• I = 80

909.

a. $9 \times 6 =$ _______ •		• F = 60
b. $54 \div 9 =$ _______ •		• C = 9
c. $4 \div 2 =$ _______ •		• G = 9
d. $6 \times 10 =$ _______ •		• H = 2
e. $90 \div 10 =$ _______ •		• A = 40
f. $6 \times 3 =$ _______ •		• D = 18
g. $4 \times 10 =$ _______ •		• B = 6
h. $30 \div 5 =$ _______ •		• J = 54
i. $64 \div 8 =$ _______ •		• E = 8
j. $45 \div 5 =$ _______ •		• I = 6

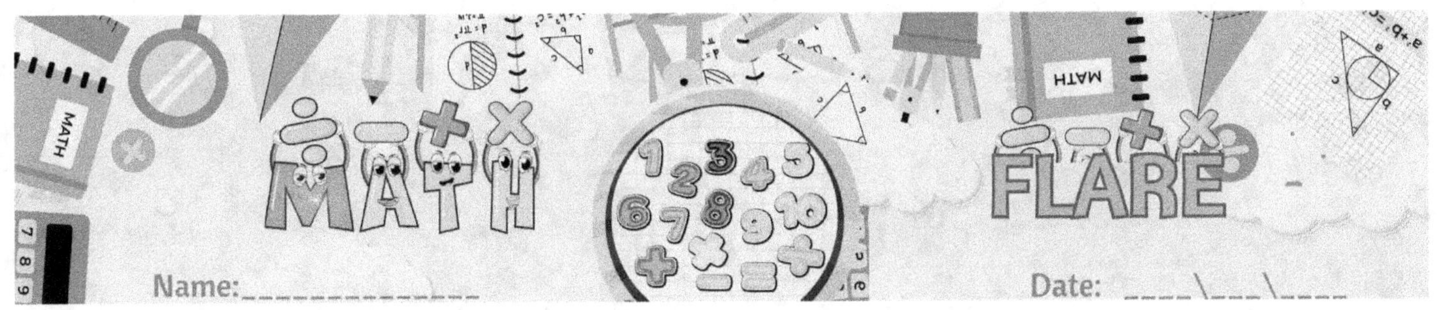

910.

a. 6 × 4 = _______ •	• D = 1
b. 10 ÷ 10 = _______ •	• J = 16
c. 4 × 1 = _______ •	• F = 56
d. 7 × 8 = _______ •	• C = 5
e. 21 ÷ 3 = _______ •	• I = 8
f. 6 × 9 = _______ •	• H = 54
g. 25 ÷ 5 = _______ •	• A = 4
h. 24 ÷ 6 = _______ •	• B = 4
i. 32 ÷ 4 = _______ •	• G = 24
j. 2 × 8 = _______ •	• E = 7

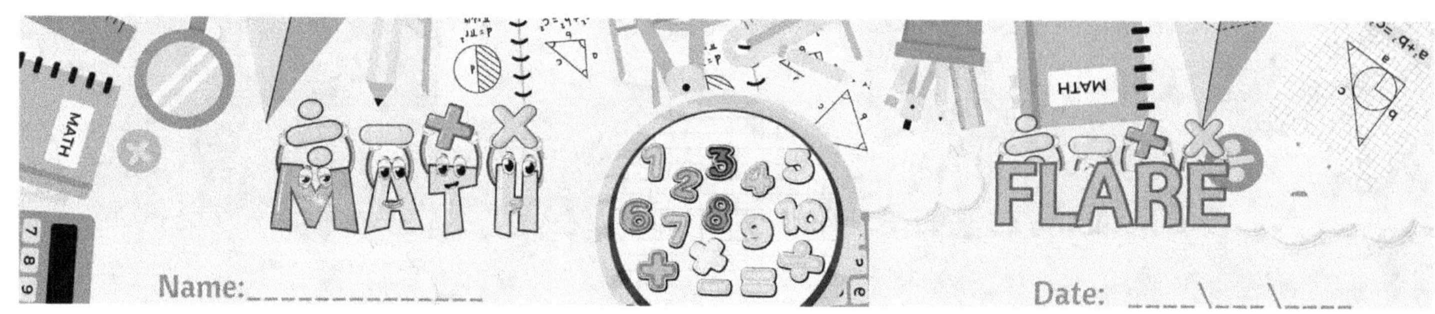

911.

a. $10 \times 3 =$ _______ •	• E = 3
b. $40 \div 10 =$ _______ •	• D = 12
c. $72 \div 8 =$ _______ •	• C = 30
d. $1 \times 3 =$ _______ •	• I = 2
e. $1 \times 8 =$ _______ •	• F = 9
f. $10 \times 10 =$ _______ •	• A = 8
g. $4 \times 3 =$ _______ •	• B = 6
h. $8 \div 4 =$ _______ •	• J = 100
i. $18 \div 3 =$ _______ •	• H = 4
j. $6 \div 2 =$ _______ •	• G = 3

912.

a. 1 × 8 = _______ •

b. 9 × 3 = _______ •

c. 7 × 7 = _______ •

d. 6 × 5 = _______ •

e. 3 × 3 = _______ •

f. 48 ÷ 8 = _______ •

g. 9 × 8 = _______ •

h. 18 ÷ 9 = _______ •

i. 72 ÷ 8 = _______ •

j. 5 × 9 = _______ •

• E = 9

• B = 8

• D = 2

• G = 49

• I = 27

• C = 72

• A = 30

• J = 45

• F = 6

• H = 9

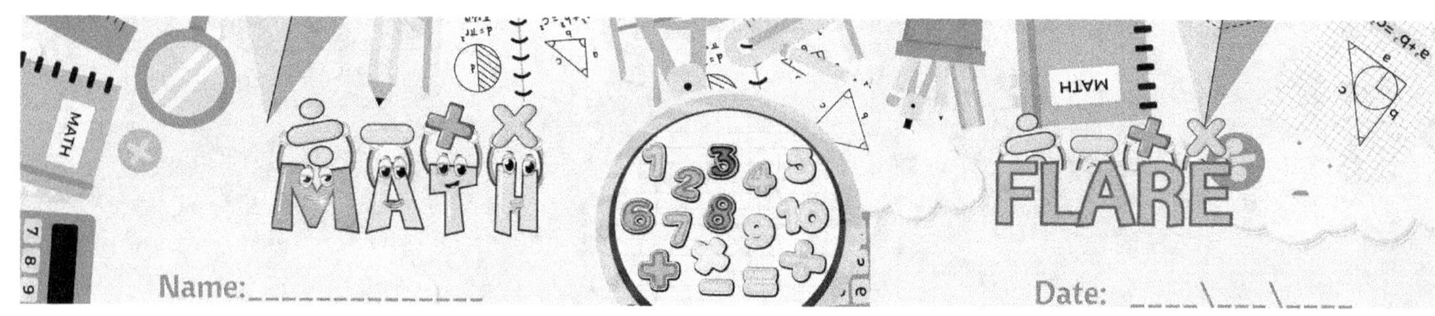

Name:______________   Date: _______________

913.

a. $10 \times 1 =$ _______ •	• F = 16
b. $8 \times 2 =$ _______ •	• E = 7
c. $80 \div 8 =$ _______ •	• H = 8
d. $48 \div 6 =$ _______ •	• I = 1
e. $21 \div 3 =$ _______ •	• D = 6
f. $63 \div 7 =$ _______ •	• A = 9
g. $4 \div 4 =$ _______ •	• B = 10
h. $8 \times 9 =$ _______ •	• C = 10
i. $7 \div 1 =$ _______ •	• J = 72
j. $48 \div 8 =$ _______ •	• G = 7

ANSWERS

Page 1:   Multiplication by 2

1. 12   2. 10   3. 8   4. 6   5. 16   6. 4   7. 14   8. 18   9. 2

10. 14   11. 16   12. 12   13. 8   14. 6   15. 10   16. 2   17. 18   18. 10

19. 4   20. 12

Page 2:   Multiplication by 3

21. 6   22. 12   23. 9   24. 24   25. 15   26. 3   27. 21   28. 27   29. 18

30. 27   31. 21   32. 12   33. 15   34. 6   35. 24   36. 18   37. 3   38. 18

39. 24   40. 12

Page 3:   Multiplication by 4

41. 32   42. 12   43. 24   44. 20   45. 16   46. 8   47. 28   48. 36

49. 4   50. 8   51. 24   52. 20   53. 36   54. 12   55. 28   56. 4

57. 32   58. 20   59. 16   60. 4

Page 4:   Multiplication by 5

61. 15   62. 45   63. 25   64. 10   65. 20   66. 30   67. 35   68. 5

69. 40   70. 10   71. 30   72. 35   73. 15   74. 40   75. 45   76. 20

77. 5   78. 10   79. 20   80. 30

Page 5:   Multiplication by 6

81. 42   82. 12   83. 54   84. 48   85. 24   86. 30   87. 36

88. 18   89. 6   90. 18   91. 54   92. 24   93. 42   94. 12

95. 48   96. 30   97. 6   98. 30   99. 6   100. 48

Page 6: Multiplication by 7

101. 7   102. 49   103. 35   104. 21   105. 14   106. 42   107. 63   108. 28

109. 56   110. 21   111. 7   112. 35   113. 42   114. 56   115. 28   116. 63

117. 14   118. 56   119. 28   120. 7

Page 7: Multiplication by 8

121. 64   122. 56   123. 24   124. 72   125. 40   126. 48   127. 16   128. 32

129. 8   130. 24   131. 56   132. 72   133. 48   134. 32   135. 40   136. 16

137. 8   138. 48   139. 32   140. 48

Page 8: Multiplication by 9

141. 54   142. 63   143. 81   144. 18   145. 27   146. 9   147. 45   148. 36

149. 72   150. 63   151. 9   152. 36   153. 45   154. 18   155. 72   156. 27

157. 54   158. 45   159. 63   160. 72

Page 9: Multiplication by 10

161. 20   162. 40   163. 50   164. 60   165. 30   166. 90   167. 70

168. 80   169. 10   170. 60   171. 40   172. 20   173. 80   174. 70

175. 50   176. 10   177. 90   178. 30   179. 60   180. 30

Page 10: Basic Multiplication

181. 24   182. 15   183. 48   184. 56   185. 63   186. 63

187. 64   188. 16   189. 72   190. 8   191. 8   192. 35

193. 70   194. 20   195. 24   196. 45   197. 40   198. 6

199. 30   200. 10   201. 12   202. 48   203. 32   204. 18

205. 90   206. 16   207. 56   208. 27   209. 10   210. 49

211. 12   212. 36   213. 40   214. 36   215. 42   216. 6

217. 54   218. 21   219. 21   220. 6   221. 72   222. 15

223. 18   224. 20   225. 3   226. 12   227. 24   228. 40

229. 4   230. 1   231. 5   232. 9   233. 14   234. 14

235. 70   236. 90   237. 24   238. 28   239. 5   240. 7

241. 8   242. 30   243. 35   244. 2   245. 30   246. 6

247. 16   248. 80   249. 42   250. 50   251. 80   252. 45

253. 60   254. 100   255. 20   256. 50   257. 4   258. 32

259. 8   260. 20   261. 28   262. 54   263. 12   264. 9

265. 81   266. 9   267. 36   268. 18   269. 2   270. 25

271. 7   272. 27   273. 4   274. 3   275. 18   276. 10

277. 10   278. 60   279. 30   280. 40

Page 15: Multiplication: 2 x 1

281. 44   282. 82   283. 62   284. 40   285. 48   286. 33   287. 88

288. 63   289. 84   290. 44   291. 68   292. 40   293. 60   294. 96

295. 24   296. 88   297. 66   298. 80   299. 99   300. 20   301. 86

302. 64   303. 86   304. 75   305. 90   306. 49   307. 50   308. 80

309. 55   310. 38   311. 89   312. 60   313. 80   314. 26   315. 27

316. 93   317. 30   318. 84   319. 47   320. 22   321. 36   322. 43

323. 35   324. 57   325. 98   326. 46   327. 71   328. 48   329. 66

330. 36   331. 39   332. 39   333. 95   334. 59   335. 69   336. 14

337. 42   338. 28   339. 93   340. 10   341. 88   342. 20   343. 90

344. 97   345. 52   346. 94   347. 48   348. 72   349. 81   350. 58

351. 29   352. 30   353. 73   354. 77   355. 42   356. 51   357. 74

358. 31   359. 92   360. 61   361. 84   362. 68   363. 50   364. 99

365. 21   366. 62   367. 54   368. 37   369. 76   370. 78   371. 32

372. 34   373. 45   374. 15   375. 16   376. 28   377. 41   378. 23

379. 63   380. 91

Page 20: Multiplication: 3 x 1

381. 808   382. 480   383. 669   384. 482   385. 666   386. 840

387. 484   388. 448   389. 622   390. 888   391. 938   392. 555

393. 693   394. 488   395. 812   396. 804   397. 688   398. 609

399. 808   400. 866   401. 636   402. 800   403. 360   404. 505

405. 440   406. 848   407. 402   408. 608   409. 528   410. 860

411. 406   412. 996   413. 963   414. 666   415. 336   416. 369

417. 101   418. 990   419. 408   420. 280   421. 333   422. 633

423. 400   424. 596   425. 668   426. 840   427. 945   428. 422

429. 404   430. 396   431. 550   432. 509   433. 390   434. 933

435. 999   436. 844   437. 639   438. 602   439. 153   440. 460

441. 466   442. 246   443. 660   444. 966   445. 300   446. 179

447. 686   448. 462   449. 826   450. 244   451. 208   452. 889

453. 339   454. 906   455. 337   456. 264   457. 204   458. 444

459. 960   460. 480   461. 500   462. 408   463. 404   464. 630

465. 884   466. 888   467. 648   468. 363   469. 484   470. 303

471. 802   472. 663   473. 617   474. 206   475. 129   476. 822

477. 884   478. 330   479. 930   480. 606

Page 25:   Commutative Property

481. 2   482. 8   483. 9   484. 5   485. 9   486. 9   487. 5

488. 10   489. 4   490. 4   491. 3   492. 8   493. 4   494. 10

495. 8   496. 3   497. 7   498. 1   499. 3   500. 8   501. 7

502. 10   503. 9   504. 8   505. 1   506. 3   507. 2   508. 10

509. 10   510. 3   511. 10   512. 6   513. 9   514. 5   515. 10

516. 7   517. 1   518. 4   519. 8   520. 5   521. 6   522. 7

523. 2   524. 8   525. 6   526. 9   527. 5   528. 5   529. 3

530. 8   531. 9   532. 7

Page 28:   Division by 2

533. 4   534. 16   535. 3   536. 9   537. 11   538. 7   539. 18   540. 2

541. 5   542. 13   543. 1   544. 15   545. 12   546. 8   547. 10   548. 17

Page 29:   Division by 3

549. 8   550. 6   551. 3   552. 11   553. 5   554. 15   555. 13

556. 12   557. 2   558. 4   559. 7   560. 17   561. 14   562. 9

563. 10   564. 18   565. 16   566. 19   567. 20   568. 1

Page 30:   Division by 4

569. 8   570. 5   571. 19   572. 14   573. 16   574. 4   575. 18

576. 1   577. 15   578. 6   579. 7   580. 11   581. 9   582. 20

583. 3   584. 13   585. 17   586. 10   587. 2   588. 12

Page 31:   Division by 5

589. 17   590. 3   591. 11   592. 1   593. 7   594. 18   595. 5

596. 13   597. 12   598. 2   599. 14   600. 6   601. 20   602. 10

603. 15   604. 19   605. 9   606. 4   607. 16   608. 8

Page 32:   Division by 6

609. 12   610. 3   611. 7   612. 6   613. 15   614. 4   615. 16

616. 2   617. 1   618. 11   619. 8   620. 17   621. 10   622. 14

623. 13   624. 19   625. 9   626. 5   627. 18   628. 20

Page 33:   Division by 7

629. 4   630. 8   631. 3   632. 12   633. 10   634. 6   635. 13

636. 18   637. 19   638. 2   639. 20   640. 17   641. 16   642. 7

643. 5   644. 15   645. 11   646. 1   647. 9   648. 14

Page 34:   Division by 8

649. 5   650. 12   651. 10   652. 8   653. 14   654. 6   655. 4

656. 2   657. 18   658. 19   659. 15   660. 11   661. 16   662. 7

663. 1   664. 13   665. 9   666. 17   667. 3   668. 20

Page 35:   Division by 9

669. 4   670. 6   671. 14   672. 16   673. 5   674. 9   675. 11

676. 2   677. 18   678. 7   679. 1   680. 10   681. 3   682. 8

683. 20   684. 17   685. 19   686. 12   687. 13   688. 15

Page 36: Division by 10

689. 1   690. 3   691. 9   692. 2   693. 15   694. 17   695. 10   696. 8

697. 7   698. 5   699. 13   700. 16   701. 12   702. 14   703. 19

Page 37: Basic Division

704. 19   705. 9   706. 16   707. 9   708. 17   709. 12   710. 20

711. 2   712. 18   713. 6   714. 4   715. 3   716. 6   717. 3

718. 7   719. 17   720. 8   721. 3   722. 13   723. 15   724. 12

725. 3   726. 15   727. 18   728. 12   729. 15   730. 3   731. 10

732. 15   733. 19   734. 13   735. 10   736. 4   737. 17   738. 7

739. 14   740. 6   741. 10   742. 5   743. 17   744. 4   745. 9

746. 6   747. 4   748. 20   749. 4   750. 7   751. 19   752. 15

753. 7   754. 14   755. 8   756. 14   757. 2   758. 11   759. 18

760. 14   761. 16   762. 13   763. 7   764. 4   765. 11   766. 1

767. 10   768. 2   769. 1   770. 16   771. 2   772. 14   773. 12

774. 3   775. 5   776. 6   777. 18   778. 17   779. 1   780. 10

781. 7   782. 12   783. 2   784. 9   785. 12   786. 2   787. 5

788. 8   789. 14   790. 17   791. 6   792. 17   793. 6   794. 10

795. 19   796. 6   797. 16   798. 17   799. 2   800. 5   801. 5

802. 20   803. 15   804. 16   805. 13   806. 9   807. 5   808. 9

809. 18   810. 7   811. 10   812. 10   813. 20   814. 11   815. 9

816. 12   817. 4   818. 18   819. 16   820. 14   821. 13   822. 12

823. 20   824. 13   825. 8   826. 6   827. 5   828. 1   829. 19

830. 17   831. 9   832. 14   833. 4   834. 3   835. 13   836. 11

837. 19   838. 3   839. 20   840. 13   841. 19   842. 20   843. 11

844. 8   845. 19   846. 2   847. 14   848. 11   849. 9   850. 15

851. 4   852. 17   853. 18   854. 15   855. 16   856. 11   857. 20

858. 13   859. 1   860. 5   861. 8   862. 12   863. 15   864. 13

865. 16   866. 18   867. 11   868. 15   869. 3   870. 16   871. 8

872. 3   873. 18   874. 2   875. 20   876. 10   877. 1   878. 11

879. 2   880. 10   881. 18   882. 19   883. 7   884. 14   885. 8

886. 4   887. 5   888. 8   889. 16   890. 1   891. 8   892. 11

893. 1   894. 5   895. 1   896. 6   897. 12   898. 9   899. 1

900. 19   901. 20   902. 7   903. 7

Page 47: Matching the answers.

904. a.F b.D c.E d.C e.G f.J g.B h.H i.I j.A

905. a.B b.H c.I d.E e.D f.C g.A h.F i.G j.J

906. a.G b.H c.E d.I e.B f.D g.C h.A i.J j.F

907. a.G b.A c.B d.E e.H f.C g.I h.D i.F j.J

908. a.J b.A c.G d.D e.H f.C g.E h.B i.F j.I

909. a.J b.B c.H d.F e.G f.D g.A h.I i.E j.C

910. a.G b.D c.A d.F e.E f.H g.C h.B i.I j.J

911. a.C b.H c.F d.E e.A f.J g.D h.I i.B j.G

912. a.B b.I c.G d.A e.H f.F g.C h.D i.E j.J
913. a.B b.F c.C d.H e.E f.A g.I h.J i.G j.D

www.ingramcontent.com/pod-product-compliance
Lightning Source LLC
Chambersburg PA
CBHW081918120726
47996CB00010B/3381